Literature in Perspective

General Editor: Kenneth Grose

George Eliot

Literature in Perspective

George Eliot

T. S. Pearce

ROWMAN AND LITTLEFIELD
Totowa, New Jersey

823.8
E42 zpe

First published in the United States, 1973
by Rowman and Littlefield, Totowa, New Jersey

© T. S. Pearce 1973

Set in 11 on 12 point Bembo and printed in Great Britain by The Camelot Press Ltd., London and Southampton

SBN 0-87471-138X

Literature in Perspective

Reading is a pleasure; reading great literature is a great pleasure, which can be enhanced by increased understanding, both of the actual words on the page and of the background to those words, supplied by a study of the author's life and circumstances. Criticism should try to foster understanding in both aspects.

Unfortunately for the intelligent layman and young reader alike, recent years have seen critics of literature (particularly academic ones) exploring slender ramifications of meaning, exposing successive levels of association and reference, and multiplying the types of ambiguity unto seventy times seven.

But a poet is 'a man speaking to men', and the critic should direct his efforts to explaining not only what the poet says, but also what sort of man the poet it. It is our belief that it is impossible to do the first without doing the second.

Literature in Perspective, therefore, aims at giving a straightforward account of literature and of writers—straightforward both in content and in language. Critical jargon is as far as possible avoided; any terms that must be used are explained simply; and the constant preoccupation of the authors of the Series is to be lucid.

It is our hope that each book will be easily understood, that it will adequately describe its subject without pretentiousness so that the intelligent reader who wants to know about Donne or Keats or Shakespeare will find enough in it to bring him up to date on critical estimates.

Even those who are well read, we believe, can benefit from a lucid exposition of what they may have taken for granted, and perhaps—dare it be said?—not fully understood.

K. H. G.

George Eliot

The novel is the most difficult literary form to criticise. The problem is made worse when the novelist is a great one. It has not been possible in this account of George Eliot's life and work to do more than concentrate on certain aspects of each of her major novels, and to try to draw out from them the most important characteristics of her work.

Middlemarch has gradually come to be regarded as one of the greatest English novels, and in recent years George Eliot's reputation has begun to pass that of all her contemporaries and many of her successors. Her novels are often difficult and require more strenuous attention than those of Jane Austen or Dickens, but her control of all aspects of the novelist's art is proportionately greater, and more rewarding to study. Recently also, features of her work which have been regarded as blemishes have been re-examined. Her characters are no longer to be seen as distorted when they are like her, a criticism levelled at Maggie Tulliver and Dorothea Brooke; it is now clear that she maintained an objective view even of these characters, especially the latter. Her so-called editorial intrusions, or author's comments, are no longer merely dismissed as misjudgments, but seen as necessary parts of what she was trying to achieve.

In her work, the novel in England reached a maturity which has not been passed.

In this book, I have tried to give a sufficient account of her life, so that her personality and the striking cast of her mind can emerge, and also some account of the novel up to the time of her first fictional writing in such a way that what she brought to the form can be perceived by contrast.

The dependence of Chapters 1 and 2 on Professor Haight's biography will be obvious, and was inescapable. His work on the novelist since the war has been the most important contribution to her reappraisal. Most of the letters quoted are from the Biography, and the page references given refer to it, since it is more generally accessible than the Collected Letters. In various other chapters, I am also indebted to the works listed in Further Reading, especially to *The Great Tradition*. I am most grateful to Mr. K. H. Grose for his advice and encouragement in preparing this book.

T. S. P.

Acknowledgements

The author and publishers are indebted to the following for permission to use illustrations: William Blackwood and Sons Ltd. for the cover photograph, the National Portrait Gallery for the photograph of the portrait by Durade, the British Tourist Authority for the photograph of Arbury Hall, the Mansell Collection for the photograph of the Phiz engraving and the British Museum for the photograph of the piece of the original manuscript of *Silas Marner*.

Acknowledgments

Contents

The Author

T. S. Pearce, M.A., is Head of the English Department, Cheltenham College. He is the author of *T. S. Eliot* in this Series.

Contents

The Author

. . . .

I

Mary Anne Evans 1819–1854

George Eliot was 'the woman who lived with Mr. Lewes'. George was *his* Christian name, and Eliot was 'a good mouth-filling, easily-pronounced word'. She used a masculine pseudonym so that her novels would not be accorded the trivial response which feminine novelists of the period received, often justly, and also to protect herself and Mr. Lewes from further scandal than was already created by their living together. From 1855 until his death in 1878 she lived with George Henry Lewes as his wife, and was known as Mrs. Lewes to those who were prepared to keep up or establish acquaintanceship with them. She helped him to care for his three sons, and indeed paid for their education from her own earnings which latterly were far in excess of her husband's. Her revenues also paid the debts incurred by Agnes Lewes, her husband's first wife. Her choice of life, taken with full awareness of the consequences, brought her a strong measure of social ostracism, which was not fully overcome until the last ten years of her life; her brother, who had severed all contact with her in 1857, only renewed it after Lewes's death, when George Eliot married, this time legally, her friend, John Cross. She rebelled also against her religious upbringing, and remained a freethinking agnostic for the rest of her life, but she never gave her name or allegiance to any doctrinaire system of ideas, and remained by temperament and perhaps habit associated with the religious faith of her childhood. She was not rebellious by nature. She liked peaceful lives, rooted in homes of long standing, in families, and in duties. She was not radical except in her passionate conviction, maintained with the utmost integrity, that she must do what was right as she saw it.

She was highly accomplished intellectually, not only as a woman in her time, but as a strong and independent mind in any time. She knew Greek and Latin, French, German and Italian. Her first work was a translation of a complex and original work on the life of Christ. She was not beautiful, rather the reverse, though she had a compelling power over those who met her, particularly on account of her voice. This compelling power, which derived from her immense imaginative sympathy for the lives of others, is what animates her novels and counterbalances the formidable resources of intellect and learning which make her forbidding as a person.

The story of her own life is more strenuous in its conflicts and more dramatic in its developments than most of the lives which her novels record, and the decisions she took, especially with regard to her faith and her view of marriage, are more socially significant of her period than any taken by her characters. It is this radical progress of her life combined with her immense sympathy for and understanding of those who led much more ordinary lives that accounts for the great breadth of characterisation and setting which her novels contain. In this respect, she was less limited than any novelist who preceded her, and with these resources, of endowments and of experience, it is not surprising that she wrote novels on the scale of *Middlemarch* and *Daniel Deronda*.

Mary Anne Evans was born on 22 November 1819 at South Farm, Arbury, just south-east of Nuneaton in Warwickshire. Her father, Robert Evans, was land agent for the Newdigate family, who lived in Arbury Hall and owned the nearby Astley Castle; he was responsible for road-building and coal-mining in the area, as well as managing the land. His first wife died in 1809 leaving two children, Robert and Fanny, and he took a second wife, Christiana Pearson, who was the youngest daughter of a well-established local family. The Evanses had three more children, Chrissey, Isaac and Mary Anne, who was named after two of her mother's sisters. In 1820 the family moved to Griff House on the Coventry road, and it is there that Mary Anne spent her childhood and formed most of her basic affections and characteristics. She remained throughout her life and in all her novels attached to the life of the countryside, and to the influence which a strong attachment to it gave, and it was in this area also that she gained, chiefly through her own close observation, the insight into the lives of ordinary provincial folk which form the greater part of her novels. She learned too how the differing areas of society fitted together through her experience in her family and at school in Nuneaton and through her father's work which brought her into contact with the more aristocratic life of the landowners. She was a very affectionate child and was strongly attached to her brother Isaac. However, in 1824, he was sent to a school near Coventry, and she to join her sister at a school in Attleborough near Nuneaton, since their mother had been unwell following the loss of twin sons in 1821. When she was nine she was sent to a boarding school in Nuneaton, where she met Maria Lewis, a young Irishwoman of strong evangelical faith. Miss Lewis introduced Mary Anne to the intense study of the Scriptures and probably developed the deep religious concern which remained a part of her temperament long after she had ceased to follow evangelical principles. Her family's attitude to religion was conventional and unquestioning, a matter of social propriety rather than involved commitment, as is revealed when she eventually brings the matter to a crisis with her father in 1842.

In 1832 Mary Anne moved to the Miss Franklins' school in Coventry so that her already noted talents might have a fuller chance of development. Here for the first time she met people from other parts of the country, and began to acquire accomplishments—music, singing and drawing—which must have rapidly enlarged her own experience, alongside her progress in conventional academic studies. Her first writings are from this time. Her essays were noted as remarkable, and she also began a work of fiction under the influence of Scott, and his inferior successor G. P. R. James, whose work she was reading in 1829–31. It was called 'Edward Neville', a story of the Royalists set in 1650, though it is not anything that would ever have been looked at again but for its author's later eminence. It is largely dependent on its source, and that source is not accurate.

Her religious preoccupations continued, but it is worth noting that she did not even then adhere to any other sectarian pattern than that in which she was brought up. There is no record of her confirmation, but on Christmas Day 1836 she joined her father and sister at Chilvers Coton Church, where she had been baptised, and took Communion. Her mother had died earlier in the year, and Mary Ann, who had now dropped the 'e' on her second name, had returned to Griff to live with her father and look after him. During this period her reading is mainly of religious works, and her letters show a strongly austere view of life which even leads her to express distaste for the whole idea of novels to her friend Maria Lewis. The catalogue of her reading is daunting, considering she is not yet twenty, though she is never buried away in her academic progress. She remains in contact with her school-friends, travels with her father, and takes pleasure in the lives of her sisters' families. Her letters show signs of her characteristic feeling of renunciation which is strong in many of her female characters, although in her own life she only renounced what would have made her unhappy, whereas her characters take courses which her own life showed to be wrong. In 1840 she wrote to a former school-friend:

> Every day's experience seems to deepen the voice of foreboding that has long been telling me, 'the bliss of reciprocated affection is not allotted to you under any form. Your heart must be widowed in this manner from the world, or you will never seek a better portion; a consciousness of possessing the fervent love of any human being would soon become your heaven, therefore it would be your curse'.
>
> HAIGHT, 27

Around the age of twenty, Mary Ann's reading began to broaden to include the Romantics, and her lasting love for Wordsworth, whose work has a strong underlying influence on her own, dates from this time. She began too to study science of all kinds, which became another influence, accounting for a great range of imagery in her novels, and probably for her easy rapport with George Lewes. She began to apply her scientific interests and attitudes to her religion and to question the superstitious basis of some aspects of her faith.

In 1841 Mary Ann and her father moved to a house on the Foleshill road near Coventry, because Isaac was to be married and to take over the house at Griff where they had lived almost all of Mary Ann's life. This move marked the end of a period in her life for in Coventry she met new friends, and soon afterwards came the dispute with her father over her religious beliefs. Through their neighbours, she was introduced to Charles and Cara (Caroline) Bray. They had a tendency to freethinking in religious matters, since Cara, at least, had a Unitarian background and her brother Charles Hennell had recently published 'An Inquiry into the Origins of Christianity', which although not very revolutionary in itself at least presupposed the possibility of questioning doctrinal matters that had not hitherto been thought open to question. Her contact with these new friends crystallised thoughts which had been developing for some time, and showed her that her evangelicalism was a false covering over her real temperament. At the beginnning of 1842 Mary Ann stopped going to church with her father and Miss Lewis. Her friendship with Miss Lewis faded from then, while her father after reproving her refused to discuss the issue. Friends attempted to persuade her that she was wrong, and her brother joined her father in an attempt to change her mind by masculine authority. Finally, on 28 February, she wrote to her father a letter which more than anything else from her early years shows the qualities of mind and sensibility which combined to create Maggie Tulliver, Dorothea Brooke, Gwendolen Harleth and Daniel Deronda. The letter deserves to be quoted in full:

Foleshill, Monday morning (28 Feb. 1842)

My Dear Father,

As all my efforts in conversation have hitherto failed in making you aware of the real nature of my sentiments, I am induced to try if I can express myself more clearly on paper so that both I in writing and you in reading may have our judgments unobstructed by feeling, which they can hardly be when we are together. I wish entirely

15

to remove from your mind the false notion that I am inclined visibly to unite myself with any Christian community or that I have any affinity in opinion with Unitarians more than with other classes of believers in the Divine authority of the books comprising the Jewish and Christian scriptures. I regard these writings as histories consisting of mingled truth and fiction, and while I admire and cherish much of what I believe to have been the moral teaching of Jesus himself, I consider the system of doctrines built upon the facts of his life and drawn as to its materials from Jewish notions to be most dishonourable to God and most pernicious in its influence on individual and social happiness. In thus viewing this important subject I am in unison with some of the finest minds in Christendom in past ages, and with the majority of such in the present (as an instance more familiar to you than any I could name I may mention Dr. [Benjamin] Franklin). Such being my very strong convictions, it cannot be a question with any mind of strict integrity, whatever judgment may be passed on their truth, that I could not without vile hypocrisy and a miserable truckling to the smile of the world for the sake of my supposed interests, profess to join in worship which I wholly disapprove. This and *this alone* I will not do even for your sake—anything else however painful I would cheerfully brave to give you a moment's joy.

I do not hope to convince any other member of our family and probably not yourself that I am really sincere, that my only desire is to walk in that path of rectitude which however rugged is the only path to peace, but the prospects of contempt and rejection shall not make me swerve from my determination so much as a hair's breadth until I feel that I *ought* to do so. From what my brother more than insinuated and from what you yourself have intimated I perceive that your establishment at Foleshill is regarded as an un-necessary expense having no other object than to give me a centre in society—that since you now consider me to have placed an in-surmountable barrier to my prosperity in life this one object of an expenditure held by the rest of the family to be disadvantageous to them is frustrated—I am glad at any rate this is made clear to me, for I could not be happy to remain as an incubus or an unjust absorber of your hardly earned gains which might better be applied among my Brothers and Sisters with their children.

I should be just as happy living with you at your cottage at Packington or any where else if I can thereby minister in the least to your comfort—of course unless that were the case I must prefer to rely on my own energies and resources feeble as they are—I fear nothing but voluntarily leaving you. I can cheerfully do it if you desire it and shall go with deep gratitude for all the tenderness and rich kindness you have never been tired of shewing me. So far from complaining I shall joyfully submit if as a proper punishment for the pain I have most unintentionally given you, you determine to appropriate any provision you may have intended to make for my future support to your other children whom you may consider more deserving. As a last vindication of herself from one who has no one to speak for her I may be permitted to say that if ever I loved you I do so now, if ever I sought to obey the laws of my Creator and to follow duty wherever it may lead me I have that determination now and the consciousness of this will support me though every being on earth were to frown upon me.

Your affectionate daughter
Mary Ann

HAIGHT, 41-3

In this letter, there is heard, more than in anything she had written before, the authentic voice of George Eliot, although the mature George Eliot might have written it with an eye to its limitations as part of a characterisation. Nevertheless the force of the prose, the complexity of the sensibility trying to accommodate all the personalities it feels to be involved, and the utter determination, not altogether free here of the charge of priggishness, to follow through a fully realised course of action despite known and painful consequences, together convey the distinctive qualities that are always present in the fuller characterisations in the novels. The letter, while it lacks the humorous detachment and objectivity which she later achieved, is surely the product of reflection and composure. It avoids self-pity, although it tends to heroics. More significantly, it avoids egoism, despite its assertion of the writer's highly personal and individual intentions, because it contains the awareness of her father's nature and likely reactions, and the awareness that others may think her wrong. The true egoist, that George Eliot later portrays so acutely in Grandcourt, seldom thinks he is wrong, or indeed bothers about what others think or feel at all.

Although Robert Evans was unrelenting, Isaac intervened and it was arranged that Mary Ann should move back to Griff for a while. Eventually she returned to Foleshill on 30 April, and two weeks after that agreed to attend church with her father as usual, while she was free to have her own thoughts during the service. This compromise does not in any sense devalue the importance of the letter to her father but rather clinches the whole experience as one which was surely of the utmost importance in forming the basis of her views on responsibility and motivation. Twenty-seven years later, in 1869, she still expressed regret at the conflict and commented on 'how much fault there is on the side of the young in such cases, of their ignorance of life, and the narrowness of their intellectual superiority'. What is revealed by this whole episode is the intensity with which George Eliot lived her life, the sincerity of her pursuit of truth, and her clear awareness of the fact that ultimately human beings with all their sensations are more important and more significant in the development of events than any ideas which motivate them.

During the next ten years, Mary Ann Evans was extending both her intellectual life and her experience of people, though the former is more superficially important, and the years pass without further crisis or epoch-making event. At the Brays she met many and various people from a richer and wider world than any she had known till then, some of them eminent, like Robert Owen and Emerson, all of them drawn from a world where Mary Ann's present frame of mind, enquiring and questing, was not the exception but the rule. In 1844 she was invited to take over the translating of David Friedrich Strauss's *Life of Christ*, the first attempt at a thoroughly historical account of Jesus as a historical figure.

The translation was published in 1846, though Mary Ann received no public credit for it, and only £20. The book had a great influence on 19th-century religious thought, and it is worth noting that Mary Ann's crisis with her father, and her subsequent work on this book occurred about fifteen to eighteen years before the publication of *The Origin of Species*.

In this period, Mary Ann also experienced some encounters

on the personal level which began to bring her out of the naïve state in which she left Griff. There was an unfortunate episode with Dr. Brabant, the father of a friend of the Brays, with whom she stayed at his home in Devizes in 1843. Although the details of what happened are not known, Dr. Brabant, aged sixty-two, obviously made advances to her, and the visit ended somewhat abruptly, at the instigation of his sister-in-law. Another episode, in 1845, although less grotesque, caused Mary Ann some passing distress. She was proposed to by a young painter and picture-restorer, and for a very short time thought seriously of the proposal. She soon realised that she would be sacrificing many of her aspirations, but a letter of the time records the effect of the incident on her conscience:

> My unfortunate 'affaire' did not become one 'du cœur', but it has been anything but a comfortable one for my conscience. If the circumstances could be repeated with the added condition of my experience I should act very differently. As it is I have now dismissed it from my mind, and only keep it recorded in my book of reference, article *'Precipitancy, ill effects of'*.   HAIGHT, 57

In 1849 Robert Evans died, after some months of ill health in which he was nursed by Mary Ann, and as a relief from this the Brays arranged a continental tour for her, the first of many she was to take later in life. They travelled in France and Italy, and arrived finally in Geneva where Mary Ann resolved to stay for the winter. Here she made a close friendship with M. and Mme. D'Albert Durade, with whom she lodged for the latter part of her stay, and M. D'Albert eventually accompanied her back to England in 1850.

After a few months of rather unsettled life in England, a third and important phase of her life begins, also marked by another change of her name. In 1851 she began to use the form Marian, which she continued to use until shortly before her death. This period of her life is dominated by her relationship with the publisher of her translation of Strauss, John Chapman, and her work with him on *The Westminster Review*, which marks the beginning of her literary career. She wrote her first article for

The Review in 1850, a review of a religious work that had arisen out of the *Life of Christ*, and stayed at Chapman's house in the Strand. This house had been built originally as a hotel, and in it he had his publishing house on the ground floor, while his wife let out the rooms on the upper floors to paying guests. Chapman was twenty-nine, married to a wife fourteen years older than himself, with three children, two of whom lived at home, and retaining a governess, Miss Elizabeth Tilley, who was in fact his mistress. Marian Evans went to lodge in this house in January 1851. Chapman rapidly developed an interest in Mozart, whose music Miss Evans was playing, and a desire to learn German. In the next two months the situation between the three women and himself deteriorated until in March Marian returned to Coventry to the Brays. For the second time, we can see that Marian is intensely involved in a situation which contributes to her experience of human behaviour, and this time in one that is decidedly unusual, in as much as the whole network of relationships was apparently known to all parties. In fact Susannah Chapman and Elizabeth Tilley seem to have united to expel Marian from a situation which they both found satisfactory. On parting from Marian, Chapman notes, 'She pressed me for some intimation of the state of my feelings,—I told her that I felt great affection for her, but that I loved E. and S. also, though each in a different way. At this avowal she burst into tears.'

Once again, Marian was the victim of her spontaneous affections, and her comparative naïvety. It seems that her idealistic enthusiasms were easily taken advantage of, and in this instance by a 'notorious philanderer'. Chapman's superficial and egoistic character surely made a considerable contribution to the creation of characters like Antony Wybrow, Arthur Donnithorne, Stephen Guest, and in a more remote way to Tito Melema, Harold Transome and Henleigh Grandcourt. However, her relationship with Chapman was by no means at an end. Later, in 1851, he became proprietor of *The Westminster Review* and invited Marian to share in the editing of it. She returned to the Strand in September, though from then on her association with Chapman remained a matter of business. In the fuller knowledge of his nature which she now had, perhaps it was not difficult for her to renounce any other sort of feeling.

During the two years in which she edited *The Review*, she came right into the centre of the currents of intellectual activity of the period. The magazine was regarded as a 'centre of enlightened radicalism', and among many other eminent and important figures she may have met Marx, and certainly met Mazzini, the architect of the Unification of Italy. She also became a close friend of the philosopher Herbert Spencer, who contributed several articles to the review. He was a sub-editor on *The Economist* and lived above its office in the Strand just opposite Chapman's house. This friendship, close as it was, showed no signs of developing into something deeper. In 1852 Marian wrote to the Brays:

> We have agreed that we are not in love with each other and that there is no reason why we should not have as much of each other's society as we like.

This remained the situation during 1852. Whatever Marian's hopes might have been they were not to be satisfied by Herbert Spencer, who also must be seen as an element in the creation of the characters of her novels whose egoism prevents them from ever engaging themselves completely in the life of another human being, a condition of life which was essential to George Eliot. Herbert Spencer, who was one year younger than Marian Evans, died a bachelor in 1903.

In 1853 Marian begins to write favourably of George Henry Lewes, whom she had met two years previously, and the final stage of the development of George Eliot has begun: 'Mr. Lewes especially is kind and attentive and has quite won my regard after having a good deal of my vituperation. Like a few other people in this world, he is much better than he seems—a man of heart and conscience wearing a mask of flippancy.' This man, who spread his talents over an immense range of activities, provided at last the stay upon which Marian Evans could finally lean, and the encouragement and support which her diffidence required to enable her to carry out her work as a novelist. Before she met him, he had worked in a notary's office and a counting-house, had studied medicine for a while, had published a popular history of philosophy, two novels, a life of Robespierre, a tragedy and numerous articles in periodicals. In 1850 he and his friend Thornton Leigh Hunt had founded a weekly newspaper called *The Leader* which had offices in Wellington Street near 142 Strand, and he also contributed to the *Westminster*. Marian grew to know him as they worked together on his articles which did not always come up to her high standards. He, like her, was notorious for his ugliness. He had married in 1841, and when Marian met him he had three sons. He and his wife had been very happily married for the first eight years, but after that Agnes Lewes began an affair with Thornton Leigh Hunt, whose son she bore in 1850. Hunt who was also married had lived for some time in what was reputed to be a co-operative household in Bayswater with other families. The Leweses were also incorrectly supposed to have lived with them, but in any case the whole group lived in an atmosphere of freethinking about social relations. It is not altogether surprising then to find that Lewes registered this child as his own, and treated him exactly as his own sons. However, his marriage did not survive the birth of a second son whose father was Hunt. In 1851 he ceased to regard Agnes as his wife, though he continued to visit her and to provide for her children for the rest of his life. He could not divorce her in the state of the law then because he had condoned her adultery in recognising Hunt's first child as his.

He and Marian came together then at a time when both were in a despondent state. During 1853 they began to see more and more of each other. She had moved away from the Strand to Cambridge Street. She started to help him with his work, at the same time as her own on the *Westminster*, and she had also begun a second important translation of Feuerbach's *Essence of Christianity* which was published in 1854. The work is a humanist work, but an additional appeal to Marian must certainly have been the ideas it contains on love and marriage:

> But marriage—we mean, of course, marriage as a free bond of love —is sacred in itself, by the very nature of the union which is therein

effected. That alone is a religious marriage which is a true marriage, which corresponds to the essence of marriage, of love. . . . Yes, only as the free bond of love; for a marriage the bond of which is merely an external restriction, not the voluntary contented self-restriction of love, in short a marriage which is not spontaneously concluded, spontaneously willed, self-sufficing, is not a true marriage, and therefore not a truly moral marriage.

ESSENCE OF CHRISTIANITY, 268

This was the only work of hers that appeared above the name of Marian Evans. On 20 July 1854 she left her lodgings in Cambridge Street, and took ship for Germany with George Henry Lewes, as his wife.

2

George Eliot 1854–1880

This decision brought on the final crisis in her life with her family and the total separation between herself and her brother which lasted until her marriage to John Cross in 1880. It also brought into her life a loneliness which because of the strength of her love for Lewes and the security of their relationship is not much noticed or recorded, but which must have been felt by both of them, and which was not broken down until the success of her novels began to make it impossible for Victorian society any longer to ignore or rebuff her.

In Cologne they met Strauss but the meeting was not a success. In Frankfurt they visited Goethe's house, since Lewes was writing a biography of him, and also the Judengasse which reappears in *Daniel Deronda*, the only one of her novels which draws fully on her experiences in Europe from this time on. They stayed in Weimar, where Lewes continued his work on Goethe, and where they met Liszt, and also Arthur Rubinstein who was the model for Klesmer in the same novel.

Meanwhile in London the storm had broken, and the couple were the subject of much rumour, some of it malicious and sensational, which affected even their close friends. Cara Bray, for example, ceased correspondence with Marian for some time afterwards. However, they were not much moved by all the fuss, as far as correspondence records, and after a stay in Berlin, where she started a translation of Spinoza's *Ethics*, they returned to England. Lewes left Marian in lodgings in Dover, while he went to London to make necessary arrangements, particularly regarding his wife and children. Marian joined him in April 1855 in rooms in Bayswater, and then they moved to East

Sheen. In September, she wrote to Cara Bray a letter which stands alongside the one to her father at the earlier crisis in 1841. This letter is less impassioned and less susceptible of criticism, but is, like the other, a remarkable expression of the strength of mind and sincere conviction on which George Eliot's decisions were based. It is printed in full in Professor Haight's biography on pages 189-91. Cara Bray began to write to Marian again after she had received it.

In May 1856 the Leweses set out for a holiday in the West Country, where Lewes could collect specimens, and work at his *Sea-Shore Studies*. The *Life of Goethe* had been published in the previous year, and it was typical of Lewes's mind that he should next turn to something so apparently remote as marine biology. Marian had finished the translation of Spinoza earlier in the year and it had been delivered to the publisher just before they left for Ilfracombe. However, the publisher was no longer interested in the work and declined to print it. Lewes recalled the manuscript, which remains, unpublished, in the Beinecke Library at Yale University.

However, something much more important for the future happened while they were on this holiday. She began to think more seriously than ever before of writing fiction and conceived the idea for her first story, *The Sad Fortunes of the Reverend Amos Barton*. When they returned to London, she first of all cleared up her magazine commitments, and then began to write *Amos Barton* in September 1856. From this time on, the record of her life is the record of her novels, and the rest of this chapter does little more than give an account of the facts of their origins and an introduction to their main features. The life of the Leweses was dominated by her writing, with Lewes himself acting as agent. Otherwise their time is taken up with Lewes's three sons, whom George Eliot helped to look after, and with extensive travelling in Europe, which they found congenial, as a help to their work, as variety, and as an escape from the pressures of English society, where for some while yet they still had a measure of notoriety. It was also necessary for them to visit Lewes's sons from time to time at their school in Switzerland. From 1854 to

1874 they made some twenty excursions to France, Germany, Italy and Spain, and this pattern in their life contributed to the objective point of view that George Eliot easily brought to English society.

She delayed communicating the news of her 'marriage' to her brother Isaac until after the completion of her first two stories. Then in May 1857 she wrote to him:

> You will be surprised, I dare say, but I hope not sorry to learn that I have changed my name, and have someone to take care of me in the world. The event is not at all a sudden one, though it may appear sudden in its announcement to you. My husband has been known to me for several years, and I am well acquainted with his mind and character. He is occupied entirely with scientific and learned pursuits, is several years older than myself, and has three boys, two of whom are at school in Switzerland, and one in England.   HAIGHT, 228

She went on then with some practical matters and enquiries about the rest of the family. A fortnight later she received a letter from Isaac Evans's solicitor requesting further particulars, which when she provided them led to the total breach between her and her brother. He never gave any sign of relenting, and in fact his eventual letter of congratulation on her marriage to John Cross is phrased coldly and formally.

Before giving an account of the production of her major works, it is important to make clear that this somewhat detailed account of George Eliot's personal development is not regarded as an essential factor in an appreciation of her work. The themes of renunciation and of guilt which are frequent in her work have at times been related to her life, with the suggestion, for example, that in creating her heroines and making them renounce happiness and prefer duty she is expiating her own sense of guilt at having done the opposite. This assessment can only arise out of a very slender grasp of George Eliot's view of duty. The decisions she took were hard ones. They involved her in actions which brought distress to herself and to others, but in taking them she followed a hard duty which for her transcended all other necessities, social or personal. This was the necessity she felt to pursue the truth of human experience at the fullest stretch of all her powers as a human being. This obliged her to forsake the habits of religion of her family, and the principles of religion of her early friends. This also led her to ignore the dangers of her decision to live openly with Lewes as his wife. These decisions indeed brought her happiness and success, but not at no cost. To assess her novels and their characters in the light of a facile interpretation of her own psychological pattern is greatly to underestimate the stature of her mind, and her very considerable self-knowledge. In creating figures like Maggie Tulliver, Romola, Dorothea Brooke and Gwendolen Harleth, all of whom in one way and another are involved in some type of renunciation leading to hardship in pursuit of certain duties thrown upon them by society or by fate, George Eliot is either examining cases which unlike herself were not able to free themselves from the chains that bound them, or cases where she could work out the consequences in human terms of such renunciations, and the motivation of them.

The purpose of revealing George Eliot's own life in such detail is to show the extent to which in some ways it transcends the lives of any of her characters, but at the same time shows how she was enabled to write of human situations more acute in their illustration of conduct and motivation than any of her predecessors, and more serious in their 'criticism of life'.

She wrote the three stories of *Scenes of Clerical Life* between September 1856 and October 1857. All three were published in monthly instalments between January and November 1857 in *Blackwood's Magazine*. Lewes carried out the necessary negotiations with John Blackwood who remained George Eliot's publisher for all her major works except *Romola*. Lewes presented the author as a clerical gentleman, and there are a few instances in the *Scenes* where the narrator is obviously delineated as a man, although these occasions are often somewhat forced. The three stories, *Amos Barton*, *Mr. Gilfil's Love-Story* and *Janet's Repentance*, are all tales of clergymen, set in and around a small Midland market town called Milby, which was soon identified as Nuneaton. The stories were well received. They excited some special interest when the locality and certain characters and situations in them were precisely identified, and there was speculation about the author, though only Dickens identified them as the work of a woman. What is more important is that the stories received marked praise and were noted as the product of a new and considerable talent, which was remarkable since the previous decade had seen the arrival of *Jane Eyre* and *Wuthering Heights*, *Vanity Fair*, *David Copperfield*, *Bleak House*, *Hard Times*, *Little Dorrit* and *Barchester Towers*, without mentioning a very large number of productions of minor talents, besides the conventional historical romances, sensational novels, and moralistic novels which appeared in hordes. Blackwood paid George Eliot £20 a month while the stories were being serialised and £180 later when he published them in book form in an edition of 1,000 copies. She earned £443 in 1857.

What immediately struck her readers was the realism with which the settings of her stories were conveyed. In introducing the stories to Blackwood, Lewes had written:

> It (the series) will consist of tales and sketches illustrative of actual life of our country clergy about a quarter of a century ago; but solely in its *human* and *not at all* in its *theological* aspect.
>
> HAIGHT, 213

In answering a query of Blackwood's about the second story, George Eliot herself wrote: 'My artistic bent is not at all to the presentation of eminently irreproachable characters, but to the presentation of mixed human beings in such a way as to call forth tolerant judgment, pity, and sympathy. And I cannot stir a step aside from what I *feel* to be *true* in character . . .' and again later: 'Art must be either real and concrete, or ideal and eclectic. Both are good and true in their way, but my stories are of the former kind. I undertake to exhibit nothing as it should be; I only try to exhibit some things as they have been or are, seen through such a medium as my own nature gives me.' These remarks give a good early idea of the bent of George Eliot's art. The three stories deal largely with ordinary incidents in the lives of mediocre individuals, which may sound dull or sententious put like that, but when handled by George Eliot even in this very early stage of her art are far from being so.

Amos Barton is the story of a narrow evangelical clergyman married to a good and devoted wife, who in his short-sighted way becomes involved, not romantically, with the widow of a Polish dancing-master who is staying locally. The village invent exotic stories about her but in fact she is as ordinary and mediocre as every other character in the tale. When her brother elopes with her maid, she descends on Amos and his wife who take her in despite their poverty and the needs of their numerous children. In due course, when Milly Barton is expecting another child, and when the strain of supporting and looking after the Countess, as she styles herself, is too much for her, her children's nurse reveals to the Countess that the gossip in the village is strongly against her and the situation in the Barton household. She departs. Milly has her child and all seems well, when her health suddenly deteriorates and she and the child die. Finally Amos is moved to another parish. The facts of the story are not exciting, but told as baldly as that do show what material the writer is concentrating on. Despite the ordinariness of the story, the people involved are real human beings with real feelings, sufferings, virtues and stupidities. Amos is foolish and learns too late. Milly loves her husband and tolerates the situation for him. The Countess and her brother are trivially and unpleasantly egoistic and selfish, and get out of the way when the going is rough. George Eliot hardly ever again wrote anything in which the characters were all so very unremarkable, so that this is a good test of her intentions and convictions, and a demonstration of the way in which her sympathies extended themselves to take in the reality of every individual.

Both *Mr. Gilfil's Love-Story* and *Janet's Repentance* include much more vigorous incident, the first a sudden death, the second wife-beating and a protracted death due to meningitis and delirium tremens; both contain romance, and the second at least has a character of markedly distinguished qualities in the Rev. Edgar Tryan. George Eliot here is trying her hand at a variety of narrative features and techniques. *Gilfil* involves some more complicated use of time, starting in about 1826 or 27, looking back to 1788 and then to 1773, and then working forward again at various speeds to 1826. *Janet's Repentance* has larger scenes of crowd activity and overall descriptions of larger areas, such as the town of Milby. Both these stories contain themes and characters, and above all character relationships which George Eliot continued to work on all through her life. At the same time, the characteristic noted then and now which most attracts critics in the stories is the strict focus on the truthful representation of the experience of ordinary people. In fact, one of Blackwood's main fears was that George Eliot was telling too much truth about Milby and the Dempsters for his readers to take.

All three stories have been charged as well with the various failings said to be typical of George Eliot, for example, the intrusive nature of her own comments into the texture of the novel, her idealistic treatment of certain characteristics, and her tendency to melodrama and conventional sentimentality. All these charges are to some extent true, especially the last, in the case of *Scenes of Clerical Life*; but it must be realised that they depend on some prior critical standard or viewpoint, the choice of which is one of the most difficult problems in making a critical judgment or evaluation of any novel. This problem is discussed more fully in Chapters 4 and 5.

Her second work, a full-length novel, *Adam Bede*, was conceived and begun very soon after the completion of *Janet's Repentance*, in October 1857. The novel is once again set in the countryside of George Eliot's childhood, though there is less opportunity for precise identification of the original scenes and characters than there was in the earlier work, and from this time on it is seldom revealing to attempt to discover the original or inspiration of any aspect of her writing. She rarely left setting or situation in an undigested or untransmuted form, and the sort of criticism which relates the finished work to its primary origin is unfruitful with George Eliot. It is more likely to produce a limitation on the critical viewpoint than an illumination, particularly in the cases where readers have identified a character as being a version of George Eliot herself. She had the type of analytical and forethinking intellect combined with considerable self-knowledge that would have easily enabled her to perceive when and in what way her material was autobiographical, and where this is the case it is reasonable to assume that it is so for a purpose other than simply recording, or 'exorcising' the author's own past experiences. For instance, there seems to be comparatively little profit to be gained by identifying the original of Dinah Morris in *Adam Bede* as George Eliot's Methodist aunt, Mrs. Samuel Evans, who seems to have resembled the fictional character in very little except in being a Methodist who preached out of doors, and who once visited a girl in prison who had murdered her own child.

Adam Bede tells of a village community, and of the intimate lives of some of its inhabitants: a carpenter of strong but also obstinate temperament, Adam Bede, his betrothed, Hetty Sorrel, a vain pretty girl who lives with the Poysers, whose farmhouse is one of the centre-pieces of the novel, and Arthur Donnithorne, the son of the local squire who falls in love with Hetty. She becomes pregnant by him, which leads her to leave home to look for him, and when she fails to find him, in a distressed condition she bears the baby but is then responsible for its death from exposure. She is condemned to death, and is visited in prison by her cousin Dinah Morris, a Methodist preacher, who helps her to come to terms with what she has done. Hetty is in fact reprieved by the last minute intervention of Arthur Donnithorne, but is transported. Finally, Adam marries Dinah.

Despite the obvious potential for melodrama which the story suggests when recorded as briefly as that, once again George Eliot concentrates on the reality of the people, the events, and the setting, and on the inter-relationships which govern their lives, the system of checks and balances which make the pattern of all lives. It is perhaps a platitude to identify this characteristic, since it is true of all novels to some extent. In the case of George Eliot it is continuously and self-consciously a major intention of hers, whereas in other writers, including such as Jane Austen and Emily Brontë, it comes fortuitously. George Eliot directs us to consider how the lives of ordinary people are shaped, how motives are related to situations and to a great many known and unknown pressures.

She prepared *Adam Bede* with great care, and wrote it more slowly than the first work. She read a good deal to acquire the proper Methodist background, and she also studied the general historical background for 1799, the year in which the novel is set. It is important to note this academic concern for correct detail here, since it applies to all her writings, and not only to such as *Romola*, *Felix Holt* and *Daniel Deronda*, which everyone recognises to be dependent on full research.

Part of *Adam Bede* was written while the Leweses were travelling in Germany, and the novel was completed in England and published on 1 February 1859. It was received with great acclaim privately and publicly. The first edition was nearly sold out in a month, and two further impressions followed directly. In June, the novel was reprinted in two volumes at a much cheaper price. Over 10,000 copies were sold in 1859, and it was translated into many European languages. It took precedence over *A Tale of Two Cities* and *The Virginians*, the current productions from the acknowledged masters Dickens and Thackeray, and on 12 April *The Times* reviewed it and said, 'It is a first-rate novel and its author takes rank at once among the masters of the art.' In May she was independently recognised by one of her friends, though by this time some others knew who George Eliot was. Barbara Bodichon, a friend from the Bray circle, wrote to her to say she had recognised Marian Evans in the writing of *Adam Bede*, and later wrote significantly: 'in it I saw her peculiar and surpassing tenderness and wisdom. I know no one so learned, and so delicate and tender' (Haight, p. 281). As the news of the authorship slowly spread, so did a certain amount of malice, which considerably hurt George Eliot, despite the fact that she had by then earned £1,200 from the book. This was little compensation for a person of her nature whose whole life heretofore had conditioned her to think very little of financial reward, and had not prepared her for the public animosity which is a necessary part of any public success. Lewes took her abroad for a short while and when they returned to news of continued success Blackwood sent her a puppy. Her reply is illuminating: 'Pug is come! come to fill up the void left by false and narrow-hearted friends. I see already that he is without envy, hatred, or malice—that he will betray no secrets, and feel neither pain at my success nor pleasure in my chagrin.'

Throughout 1859 she had been writing her next, and for a long time most famous, novel, *The Mill on the Floss*. This is the story of the Tulliver family of Dorlcote Mill near St. Oggs, a northern market town, and especially of Maggie Tulliver, a highly sensitive and intelligent girl who cannot in any way find an outlet for her true nature. She is loved by a schoolfriend of her brother's, Philip Wakem, whose love she does not fully return, but later in the novel is involved with Stephen Guest who is betrothed to her cousin Lucy. They, partly by intent and partly by accident, find themselves together overnight away from home, but Maggie rejects the consequences of this compromising situation, and returns to St. Oggs, where she meets malice and scorn. The novel also records the feud between her father and Philip's father. Maggie's father mismanages his financial affairs and is obliged to sell the Mill which is bought by Wakem. Subsequently, when Tulliver has paid off all his debts, he brutally assaults Wakem. Tom Tulliver, Maggie's brother, of whom she is deeply fond, inherits the feud, and this leads him to quarrel with Maggie over Philip, but all these issues are brought to a cataclysmic and unsatisfactory end when a violent and disastrous flood destroys the Mill, and drowns Maggie and Tom who are united in death. It is impossible to avoid the extensive conventional melodrama of several parts of this novel, and the end indeed is for many readers as bad as it sounds. At the same time the novel contains what is by far the finest of George Eliot's social observation so far, especially in her very broad presentation of Maggie's childhood, and her mother's family, the Dodsons, the three married sisters Glegg, Deane and Pullett. Here for the first time, George Eliot spreads her extensive vision over a complex society bound by underlying standards but illuminated by immense personal variety. She did not repeat this type of writing again until *Middlemarch*, and the vaster canvas of that novel meant that even there she did not do it so incisively.

The novel also contains in Maggie's decision to return to St. Oggs, even though she is compromised, the first example of George Eliot's dealing with a character in a state of crisis comparable in some ways to her own rather profounder crises. Maggie's crisis is explicitly social; it is not bound up with any deeper philosophical issue, and its nature is cuttingly satirised in George Eliot's analysis of what the 'tolerable' social reaction would have been if Maggie had in fact gone off with Stephen Guest. (See Chapter 6.) Maggie's relationships with Philip Wakem and with Stephen also provide George Eliot with her first opportunity to create situations involving sensitive and cultured people, and the characterisation of Maggie and Philip foreshadows the later achievements.

The choices that Maggie makes not only deprive her of possible happiness with either Philip or Stephen, but the second brings down on her greater unpleasantness when she returns to St. Oggs than she would have had if she had eloped. In the passages which recount how she reaches her decision, George Eliot writes for the first time in the voice which is most completely hers, the voice of deeply introspective moral discrimination. It is this voice which is most often criticised as the one in which the novelist is self-indulgent. At the same time it is the most memorable and distinctive voice in all her work. It appears sometimes as the inner voice of certain characters, and sometimes as the voice of the author herself interpreting or commenting on the situations of her characters. It is technically criticised because by being there it breaks the objectivity to which the greatest creative art must be thought to aspire. And yet, one might ask, how far is this objectivity ever achieved, and may it not be a kind of critical blindness to complain of its absence when what is present in its place is a manifestation of a mind and personality so penetrating and capacious as George Eliot's was?

The Mill on the Floss was finished at great speed in March 1860, the whole of Volume Three having been written in eight

34

weeks, and a very satisfactory financial arrangement had been secured with Blackwood, though her financial affairs were more complicated now, and she received offers from other publishers. Within three weeks of publication, the novel had sold about 5,600 copies, which was said to be unequalled since Scott's Waverley novels. The Leweses meanwhile were travelling again, this time to Italy, where George Eliot conceived the daunting project, daunting because of her immensely high standard of detail and accuracy, of her next major novel *Romola*, a story of the life of Florence in the time of Savonarola. Before this, however, she wrote her short novel *Silas Marner*, which marks the turning point in her creative life. In setting and tone it is not far from the earlier work, but it is much more obviously controlled in narrative form and in that sense marks a development, and also it introduces a certain type of theme which recurs in most of the later novels, the question of obligations and affections owed to those who have brought you up whether they are your true family or not. This is a major narrative theme of *Silas Marner*, *Romola*, *Felix Holt* where it has a double application, and *Daniel Deronda* where it has a much more varied and flexible application. She completed *Silas Marner* in March 1861 and it was printed as a one-volume novel in the same month. Short as it was, it earned her nearly £2,000 in 1861. *Silas Marner* has a close kinship with *Amos Barton* and *Adam Bede*. It is the story of a weaver who is somewhat of an outcast from his local community for his close and miserly ways. One day his hoard of money is stolen from him. Some time later miraculously he finds a baby girl at his hearth. He brings the child up as his own, but later her origins emerge. She proves to be the illegitimate daughter of the son of a local landowner, Godfrey Cass, whose brother had stolen Silas's money. When he finds this out he offers the child, Eppie Marner, the chance of regaining her rightful place, but she remains true to Silas and will not leave him. The story obviously has elements of the fairy-tale about it, but it is free from false sentiment, and George Eliot's control of the plot is sound. Silas, like Amos, is a man with very little to endear him to the reader or to those around him in the story. However, George Eliot induces a real sympathy for his sufferings and shows the regenerative power of human affection alongside the destructive force of the lust for monetary gain.

During 1861 the Leweses set out again for Italy to gain further detail for *Romola*. This time they stayed there two months, and George Eliot went on studying for the novel throughout the rest of the year, although she became despondent about it because she kept thinking of an English novel instead. At last she started in 1862.

Romola is a mixture of fiction and fact. The setting, the broad historical events, and the character of Savonarola are factual, the intimate story of Romola and Tito Melema are invention, although there is no feeling of inconsistency between the two elements. The extensive spread of the story and the display, excessive to many readers, of detailed background information make it difficult to give any idea of the subject of the novel in brief terms. It relates the history of Republican Florence at the time of its decline under pressure from neighbouring states in Italy. After the failure of the Medici rule, the monk Savonarola takes action to re-establish the republic chiefly by the creation of a band of young men responsible for the restoration of moral fibre in the city, which had been sapped by the Medici. The private story interwoven with this is of Tito Melema, a talented young Greek, who, arriving penniless in Florence, soon establishes himself through a combination of charm and talent as an important figure in the Florentine political world. He marries Romola di Bardi, the daughter of a scholar of great repute and respect. As Melema pursues his political career, he becomes hardened to the acceptance of certain manipulations of both truth and right, particularly with regard to the man Baldassare Calvo, who brought him up in Southern Italy and gave him all his skills. He is pledged to seek out Baldassarre who has been captured and imprisoned by the Turks, but he fails in this because he is comfortable where he is, and he denies Baldassarre when the latter eventually reaches Florence and confronts him. With Tito's hardening, his marriage to Romola decays and she is driven, or drawn, to Savonarola, especially since her brother had earlier espoused Christianity and broken with the family. She plans to leave Tito but is directed back to him by Savonarola as a matter of duty. The novel ends with Tito's death at Baldassarre's hands and Savonarola's execution.

The story as such is a great one. It is of epic proportions, and there are times when the novel reads as the scenario of an extensive glamorous film of the last fifteen years, preferably of the type directed by Zeffirelli. Anyone fond of such atmospheres must enjoy much of *Romola*, although it has not perhaps much of the Renaissance zest and exuberance. The characters are invested with the family likeness of all George Eliot's, and there are the same themes—the consequences of social and personal obligations when upheld, and when broken. Tito, in particular, represents the most remarkable new ground here, a man who gradually loses his immense charm as little by little he gives way to his persistent weakness of taking the easiest way out. Although he is really less subtle than them, he is the first of a line of characters which includes Harold Transome and Matthew Jermyn from *Felix Holt*, Bulstrode from *Middlemarch* and Grandcourt from *Daniel Deronda*. Lastly, in *Romola* she deals in much more detail with the type of obligation where a family relationship is not based on a blood relationship, in this case Tito's obligation to Baldassarre. The novel is a triumph of intellectual control, but for most 20th-century readers it is now a dead triumph.

For this novel, George Eliot received even more generous offers than she had for *The Mill on the Floss*, and she eventually sold it to *The Cornhill* magazine for £7,000 to be printed in twelve monthly parts, illustrated by Frederic Leighton, later President of the Royal Academy, who knew Italy well. The first instalment appeared in July 1862, when only three parts had been completed. She was not at rest while writing this novel, and what is more there had, not surprisingly, been a breach with Blackwood about which she was hardly comfortable. She finished the novel in June 1863, having extended it to fourteen instalments. In passing, in May, she noted in her journal 'Killed Tito in great excitement!' Anthony Trollope perhaps made the best common-sense criticism; he suggested she should not 'fire too much over the heads of her readers. You have to write to tens of thousands, and not to single thousands,' but he admired the 'descriptions of Florence,—little bits of Florence down to the last door-nail, and great facts of Florence up to the very fury of life among those full living nobles'. The novel was not a great success either as a serial or when it was issued in three volumes in 1863.

She began *Felix Holt—The Radical* in 1865, after a period in which she had thought about writing a play, and worked on some ideas which reappeared later in her poetry. In this new English novel, she returned to the Midlands and was able to get on more easily, though part of her theme nevertheless required considerable study such as she had given to *Adam Bede* and *The Mill on the Floss*. The novel is set at the time of the First Reform Bill, and has as a centre-piece the election riots of 1832, in which the 'hero' Felix Holt becomes involved. Like *Romola*, the novel has a public and a private theme. The public theme is political and concerns the contrast between Felix Holt, a working-class idealistic radical, and Harold Transome, a land-owning political radical, and the outcome of Harold's election campaign during which Felix takes issue with him over his methods.

Against this background is the story of the Rev. Rufus Lyon, and his step-daughter Esther, who has been brought up as his daughter; and the private story of Harold Transome, who, unknown to himself, is not the son of old Mr. Transome, but the son of the lawyer Jermyn, who has managed the Transome estates while Harold has been away in Turkey. At a crucial point in the story this knowledge is revealed to him. These two plots are brought together by a complicated mystery story uncharacteristic of George Eliot, whereby it eventually transpires that Esther Lyon is the real heir to the Transome estates. Harold's mother swallows her pride and attempts unsuccessfully to effect a marriage between Harold and Esther, but she, like Eppie Marner, prefers to remain true to her upbringing. The complexity is one of the consequences of George Eliot's work on *Romola*, as is the presentation of the riots, in which there are scenes on a grand scale such as she had not attempted before. The themes of the novel are also more complex and there is one character who like Tito in *Romola* represents a new type: Mrs. Transome, Harold's mother, for some readers one of George Eliot's finest achievements up to this time. She is extremely memorable.

The novel took only a year to write. It was published by Blackwoods to whom she happily returned when *The Cornhill* refused the new novel. She was paid £5,000 for it. It was very well received but did not sell as well as some of her earlier work, although a two-volume edition was produced six months after the first.

In 1867 the Leweses travelled to Spain, and George Eliot was working on her never very successful and now forgotten poetry. *The Spanish Gypsy* was published in 1868. It was quite highly commended, but as a poet she was derivative of her eminent predecessors, and her themes are only now interesting in that they reappear slightly in *Daniel Deronda*; however, her reputation as a novelist brought quite high sales and she earned over £1,000 for it in due course. By this time, it is perhaps worth noting that the Leweses were altogether acceptable in the best society. The Queen had read and greatly admired *Adam Bede*, they had dined in exalted circles, and their house, The Priory, on Regents Canal, to which they had moved in 1863, had become a busy centre of intellectual activity.

She began *Middlemarch* in 1869, starting with the town story of the Vincys and Featherstones. Then she began another story in 1870 called 'Miss Brooke,' and eventually decided, fortunately in the event, to combine the two. The work, which was published in eight books at two-monthly intervals, was completed by September 1872. It brought its author some £9,000, but more than that it brought her immense critical acclaim which it has continued to do. It absolutely confirmed her world-wide fame. She began to receive letters which contained remarks of this kind: 'You, who are a great lady yet know so well how all the little fishes struggle, may smile a moment at my folly which dares to love you for your goodness and inspiring handiwork,' and 'Life has come to such a pass,—now that there is no longer any God or any hereafter or anything in particular to aim at,— that it is only by coming into contact with some other person that one can be oneself. . . . And you seem now to be the only person who can make life appear potentially noble and interesting without starting from any assumptions.' The vast scale of both *Middlemarch* and *Daniel Deronda* makes it unsuitable as well as impossible to attempt an introduction to them of the kind that has been possible with the other novels in this chapter, and both receive detailed treatment in later chapters. They are George Eliot's major achievements in which all her experience is drawn together to create works which extend the range of the English novel both in breadth and depth further than anything before them. To Dickens's breadth she added psychological penetration, and to Jane Austen's and Emily Brontë's moral and psychological insights she added a range and reality of characterisation and setting scarcely equalled since.

Daniel Deronda, the last of George Eliot's novels, was started in 1874. It is the only one of her novels set in or near the period when it was written. It is set in 1865–6 and in various parts of England and Europe. It is also the only one which draws on her by then extensive experience of customs and mores which are not English. It also ventures into a field which might perhaps be seen in some ways as George Eliot's handling of another potentially explosive problem for one of its major themes is the future of the Jewish race and the possibility of a new Israel. In treating this theme with the sympathy characteristic of all her work, she is undertaking something a little akin to her own crises, of religion in 1841–2, and of social appearances in 1853. The Jewish theme of *Daniel Deronda* has never been well received, sometimes for wholly wrong reasons, but more recently because it is generally too polemical to be acceptable in a novel. What is quite certain is that it was above all the Jewish theme that engaged her on the novel and which probably accounted for the decisions about the timing and placing of the scenes. She had known from 1866 to 1868 an intelligent and unorthodox Jew, Emmanuel Deutsch, who came to The Priory frequently, and introduced her forcibly to the Zionist cause. He made an excursion to Palestine, and later to Egypt, where he died of cancer. He is certainly transmuted into the Jewish visionary

Mordecai in the novel. Much of the English part of the book is set this time in Wiltshire, not in Warwickshire, and as always she did her homework. In 1874 the Leweses stayed in Devizes and made excursions in the surrounding countryside. She called the area Wessex, though there is no direct evidence that she had this from Thomas Hardy, whose *Far from the Madding Crowd* was being serialised at the time.

Daniel Deronda was published in monthly instalments from February to September 1876, by which time George Eliot was commonly known as the greatest living English novelist. She completed one more work, a set of essays called *Impressions of Theophrastus Such*, published in 1880. The last essay in it is a fascinating sidelight on her interest in the Jewish cause.

In November 1879, after a short illness, George Lewes died. Marian was desolate. For a week she would see no one but Lewes's son, Charles, and her maid. She found some consolation and immediate purpose in finishing the last volume of Lewes's current work, and only after that was finished in early January did she show any signs of communicating with the outside world again. Eventually she was able to turn to her close friend, John Cross, whom she had known for some years and who had lately been managing her finances. In March she started to see all her old friends again, but during the year she leant more and more on Cross. Another old friend and co-architect with Lewes in her great achievement, John Blackwood, had died in October 1879. Eventually she decided to marry John Cross who had pressed her to do so several times since Lewes's death. All her life she needed a man to lean on and had in an immense variety of ways always had one: Robert Evans, Charles Bray, John Chapman, Herbert Spencer, George Lewes and John Cross. She and Cross were married in May 1880. He was twenty years younger than her. To the end she took decisions of noted unorthodoxy, although this one was orthodox enough to elicit at long last a note from her brother Isaac. Jowett's letter from Balliol said much more:

You know that you are a very celebrated person, and therefore the world will talk a little about you, but they will not talk long and what they say does not much signify. It would be foolish to give up actual affection for the sake of what people say.   HAIGHT, 42

The Crosses travelled in Italy during the summer, and a strange incident occurred in Venice when Cross, in a sudden fit of mental depression, jumped into the Grand Canal. He recovered and such an episode never occurred again, but there is some suggestion that the event affected Marian adversely. Once they were back in England, her health began to fail. In September she had another attack of an old kidney complaint, and on 22 December 1880 she died of a heart attack.

Her most memorable epitaph is the often-quoted description by F. W. H. Myers of his meeting with her in the Fellows' Garden at Trinity College, Cambridge:

> She stirred somewhat beyond her wont, and taking as her text the three words which have been used so often as the inspiring trumpet-calls of men,—the words God, Immortality, Duty,—pronounced, with terrible earnestness, how inconceivable was the first, how unbelievable the second, and yet how peremptory and absolute the third. Never perhaps have sterner accents affirmed the sovereignty of impersonal and unrecompensing law. I listened, and night fell; her grave majestic countenance turned toward me like a sybil's in the gloom; it was as though she withdrew from my grasp, one by one, the two scrolls of promise, and left me the third scroll only, awful with inevitable fates. And when we stood at length and parted, amid that columnar circuit of the forest-trees, beneath the last twilight of starless skies, I seemed to be gazing like Titus at Jerusalem, on vacant seats and empty halls,—on a sanctuary with no Presence to hallow it, and heaven left lonely of a God.
>
> HAIGHT, 464

That is well written, and George Eliot's view of life was ultimately as stern as that: there is slender comfort in her writings except for the deluded. And yet the more touching epitaph remains the letter from the young man in California which says:

> You, who are a great lady yet know so well how all the little fishes struggle, may smile a moment at my folly which dares to love you for your goodness and inspiring handiwork.   HAIGHT, 447

3

England and Europe

George Eliot was born three months after the Peterloo massacre, an event which symbolises the period of social unrest and social change during which she lived. As she in the crises of her own life demonstrated in personal terms the changing attitudes to religion and to social behaviour, so the major historical events both in England and on the Continent show a similar turmoil in public life. Although most of her novels are set in England in the early years of the 19th century, in other words in the times and places of her childhood, she herself was in later life cosmopolitan, living as much on the Continent as at home, and must have had her own searching and radical outlook confirmed by the upheavals in Europe as much as by the political changes at home.

Even in *Daniel Deronda*, which is set both later and in wider areas, one is not conscious of George Eliot as a historian, despite her close attention to historical detail. She is always chiefly concerned with the personal life in relation to its immediate social setting and to certain absolute values, but one feels that this frame of mind was in part created by the fact that she lived through a time in which superficially stable values were rapidly changing, thereby thrusting personal and individual values into a place of greater importance. Even for example in *Romola*, the most ostentatiously historical work, there is a sense in which she is still chiefly interested in the personal crises, of Tito, of Romola herself, and of Savonarola, more than in the historical development of Florence in the late 15th century. The reality of that Florence has the same universal and eternal quality as the reality of St. Oggs, or Hayslope, and the moral and spiritual issues are equally universal. The actual historical background of

George Eliot's own life then is not of the first importance except as a period of great change and of serious searching for new and better values in all areas of social life.

18th-century England was a period of comparatively little change except towards the end with the rapidly increasing influence of the new technological discoveries and of the French Revolution. In 1714 the population of the country was around five and a half million. There were no more than a dozen towns with over 50,000 inhabitants. There was a great deal of crime, which was very severely dealt with, and a great deal of squalor. At the same time there was a great deal of superficial elegance in the small society of the wealthy landowners, and the culture of London. The lack of change throughout the century is possibly best indicated by the comparatively slight changes in architectural taste from the time of Wren, through the middle period of Adam, and the Woods of Bath, to the Regency. Despite a great deal of experiment in detail and in superficial appearance, all the major building schemes (of which there were many) are of comparatively simple but imposing classical lines. There was a similar lack of change both in the squalor of the towns and in the torpor of the country society. The active body of men in public life was very small indeed, and politics were largely a matter of clans and factions.

It is in fact this world which enthralls George Eliot in many ways, rather than the world of acute change which she herself moved in. Writing in 1856 and later she turns chiefly to the rural England of the local squire, the parson, the churchwarden, the freeholding farmer and the tenant farmer, and the artisan in various walks of life, miller, weaver, carpenter. These are the basic elements of the world of *Adam Bede*, where the Coming-of-Age of the Squire's heir is a big occasion, where there is a self-evident rift between the Squire and Parson, and the rest of the village, and where there is very little consciousness of what is going on in the rest of the world at all. And they are also the basic elements of *Silas Marner*, *Felix Holt* and *Middlemarch*, although the last two are set at the time of the First Reform Bill of 1832, which is usually seen as marking the point of change between the old society and the new. Nevertheless, the lives of Brooke, Chettam and Featherstone belong to the older world; and whereas Ladislaw and Lydgate belong to the new, they never have the same rooted solidity of life which in some ways George Eliot recreates better than anything else, even though in her analysis of the moral crises of the individual lives she leaves us more favourably disposed towards the people of the new world than of the old.

That old world did, of course, begin to change during the 18th century. Most significant were the changes in technology, transport and industrial organisation which revolutionised the methods and rate of production in many areas. Weaving was quite altered by the invention of the water frame, the jenny and the mule between 1769 and 1779, and during the same period there were equally marked changes resulting from more extensive use of iron, and then of steam power. The first iron ship was made in 1787, steamboats were used in 1801 and steam locomotives in 1815. In agriculture, similar developments improved production, and there was rapid development of enclosure. In towns there was fuller administration leading to the provision of lights, roads and a police force; and the improvement of hygiene, the control of disease and the availability of cheap cotton clothes led to rapid population growth, so that the population of the country in the early 19th century was double that of 100 years before. Working conditions did not, however, improve despite the growing sense of progress and expansion that took place from 1760 to 1800, and the more fundamental social reforms had to wait until after the end of the Napoleonic wars.

In 1815 Britain had a Tory government under Lord Liverpool which was reactionary and repressive. The laws against crime were very severe so that a man could be hanged for many minor offences. Industrial working conditions were still bad and agricultural labourers were no better off with agriculture in the hands of the big landowners. In 1817 the government suspended Habeas Corpus, and it was not altogether surprising that the situation led to an incident such as the Peterloo massacre, which is only one of a series of riots in many parts of the community during the first thirty years of the century. The pressure for change came from various radical sources inspired by the American and French Revolutions and by such writers as Tom Paine, Adam Smith, Bentham and the two Mills. Their ideas were propagated in societies and magazines, and the Peterloo massacre was a result of this spread. An enormous meeting of working-class reformers in the weaving industry was organised to meet in St. Peter's Fields in Manchester with the intention of discovering how best to bring about changes in the form of representation in the House of Commons. The meeting was in the view of some eye-witnesses perfectly orderly and was quite improperly and brutally broken up by the militia after the most perfunctory reading of the Riot Act. Others reported that there was provocation and disorderly behaviour. In other words it was a typical 'demo' in which harm was done as a combination of the insecure control of the organisers over the various parts of the meeting, which may have numbered 60,000 people, men, women and children, and the extreme nervousness of the authorities who were no doubt convinced that there would be disorder, and acted accordingly whether it had actually occurred or not. Eleven people were killed, many hundreds wounded, and the incident electrified the nation. The government introduced the Six Acts designed to strengthen their repressive powers by forbidding military training and the possession of arms, and curbing the freedom of the press and its power of circulation, and reinforcing the regulations against 'seditious meetings and assemblies'. The Six Acts, however, were a last repressive fling before the combined pressure of radical opinion outside parliament and Whig pressure for more moderate gradual reform inside parliament began to take effect.

The Peterloo massacre is worth more detailed consideration in this context because of George Eliot's remarkable re-creation of a public riot in *Felix Holt*. Of the well-known historical riots of the period, the Peterloo massacre is perhaps the most famous, though it is only one of many, all of which probably have a similar pattern, being a consequence of radical thought inflaming popular and oppressed opinion brought into contact with reactionary and unimaginative, although perhaps basically inoffensive, authority. The riots in *Felix Holt* show a very similar pattern, and it is quite clear that George Eliot is not really studying the Reform Bill riots from a strictly historical viewpoint, but from a philosophical viewpoint to show as far as possible what happens when a crowd gets out of hand. In doing this, her capacity for retaining an intense control of detail while never losing the broad sweep of the action is better shown than anywhere else.

Within the fifteen years following the Peterloo massacre a great many social and political reforms were under way. The Corn Laws were repealed in 1828, the Police Force begun in 1829, the Factory Act brought in in 1833, the Test and Corporation Acts were repealed in 1828, and the Roman Catholic Relief Act brought in in 1829. The Poor Law Amendment Act came in in 1834, slavery was abolished in 1833, and most important of all the First Reform Bill was passed in 1832. Seen in the context of all the other reforms, this Act is only an important part of a general movement of reform resulting from the great upheavals of the previous sixty to eighty years, and yet it remains of special interest because it begins to make real inroads into the privilege of the landed classes which was what had sustained the absence of political change in the previous century. When seen in detail the changes introduced in the bill seem slight. The electorate was increased from 435,000 to 652,000, and there was only a modest spread of representation into the cities, although a large proportion of the rotten boroughs disappeared. However, the Act marked more than anything else the capacity of the constitution to survive change of this kind and therefore paved the way for the Second and Third Reform Acts, and for the whole process towards the ideal of one man, one vote, which was a basic demand of the radical innovators. During the thirties, the impetus of social change focused on the Chartists. In 1836 the London Working Men's Association was founded, and two years later it drew up the Charter which called for Equal Representation, Universal Suffrage, Annual Parliaments, the removal of property qualifications, Vote by Ballot, and control of the sitting and payment of M.P.s. Petitions were organised in 1839, and again in 1842 and 1848, and on the last two occasions the country developed an atmosphere of revolution. Arrests and trials became common and there were again clashes between the reformers and the authorities which led to violence. Further practical reform did not in fact arrive until the Second Reform Act of 1867 brought in by Gladstone after the death of Palmerston who had operated as a check until then. This Act further redistributed the seats, removing members from boroughs with less than 10,000 inhabitants, making new seats, and extending the franchise to increase the electorate by 938,000 voters. By this time the whole process of reform was under way, and the country began to turn to a consciousness of its new and commanding prosperity in the world. The uneasiness of the years from 1815 to 1850 gave way to a sense of great material prosperity, growing industrial production and foreign trade, and a satisfaction which was perhaps responsible for the slowing pace of reform. But it gave way also to a time of order which made it possible for much great writing to be done. The novel is eminently the literary form of a settled and peaceful time. It needs time for writing and time for reading, and this is what the prosperous Victorians had. From 1847 to 1867 there appeared an astonishing wealth of great novels, from the Brontës, from Thackeray and Dickens, from Trollope and Mrs. Gaskell, from Meredith and from George Eliot. Some twenty-five novels from these authors are still classed as major works, not including the later works of Meredith and George Eliot.

The same prosperity also made possible a much more stringent and searching type of social criticism, much more articulate than that of the active radicals of the earlier years, such as came indirectly from Dickens, and directly from Arnold and Carlyle. The century is marked by the combination of complacency and conscience, basically directed towards the improvement of the physical conditions of life, the creation of comfort and the means of happiness in the material sense. This is something which scarcely enters George Eliot's novels at all. She is not, as Dickens and Thackeray and Trollope are, a novelist of the Victorian period. She is not describing the state of life which she sees around her, and this is as true of *Daniel Deronda*, which is at least set in the mid-Victorian period, as it is of the earlier novels. Her novels are all creations of an imagination which was not tied to a specific time or place.

The history of religion during the period which influenced George Eliot requires as close study as any other facet of the history of the time. Besides the technological changes of the 18th century, the other powerful influence for change was the figure of John Wesley, and the effect he had on the church and on religious practice in general. He is important in one special way with regard to George Eliot, for the figure of Dinah Morris in *Adam Bede* who is a Wesleyan preacher, outside the framework of the church, and in another way because Methodism lay behind the Evangelicalism which affected Marian Evans so strongly in her years at Nuneaton.

Dr. David Thomson's summary of the state of religious affairs in the mid-Victorian period is very useful in helping to place George Eliot.

> The most generally accepted and practised form of Christianity at the time was that which may be broadly called evangelicalism, with its emphasis upon moral conduct as the test of the good Christian. In this sense it transcended all barriers of religious sect, and marked the religious outlook of a Quaker like Bright and of a High Church-man like Gladstone, a Low-Church Tory like Shaftesbury and a Presbyterian like Livingstone. It even colours the outlook of an agnostic like T. H. Huxley and a man like Disraeli, who although Jewish by race was a practising Christian. Its basis was biblical. Bible-reading in the home was as popular as sermonising in church. Its highest virtue was self-improvement. Its emphasis lay not on sacraments or ritual, but on organised prayer and preaching and on strict observance of Sunday. Until the 1870's this form of religion and religious worship remained the normal form for the great mass of Englishmen, although they remained divided formally into Anglicans, Methodists, Presbyterians, Quakers and the many other nonconformist sects. It was the period when the so-called 'non-conformist conscience' permeated English life and manners—even among conformists. Gradually it was weakened by the growth of

free-thinking and rationalist movements connected with the development of scientific thought, by the growth of facilities for luxury and pleasure and of greater indulgence in these facilities, and by the more ritualistic, Anglo-Catholic movement connected with the names of John Henry Newman and Edward Pusey.

ENGLAND IN THE 19TH CENTURY, CH. 5

George Eliot fits into this picture as a fervent evangelical who later became a free-thinking agnostic, with strong links through Lewes and Spencer with the development of scientific thought. The whole body of her work is permeated with a characteristic Victorian preoccupation with moral conduct.

EUROPE

The history of 19th-century Europe is dominated by the emergence of nationalism, especially the new unified nations of Germany and Italy. The process follows a pattern similar to that in England for a time, and then owing to totally different economic conditions veers away towards a much more autocratic form of nationalistic rule.

After the settlement of the Congress of Vienna in 1815 there was peace in Europe for thirty-nine years, only interrupted by minor revolutions similar in character to the disturbances in England at the same time, disturbances that sought greater democratic representation for the people. The first series occurred between 1830 and 1833 and was widespread throughout the continent. In France, the reactionary King Charles X was forced to abdicate in favour of the Duke of Orleans who was proclaimed king as Louis-Philippe; Belgium became an independent nation; there was civil war in Spain and Portugal, a new liberal constitution in Switzerland, and revolts in Germany, Italy and Poland, which were vigorously suppressed; Polish intellectual leaders were driven into exile.

The second series occurred in 1848, the so-called Year of Revolutions, and coincidentally the year of publication of the Communist Manifesto. There was rebellion in Sicily, which was followed by riots in all large Italian cities, and further disturbances occurred in Germany, France, Austria, Hungary, Switzerland and Belgium. The outcome was the end of the rule of Metternich in Eastern Europe and the destruction of feudalism. In Italy, there was a new liberal constitution in some states. In France, the Second Republic was created. In Germany, a preliminary German assembly was created. The Czechs did not succeed in making any progress. Their revolt in Prague was crushed in five days. The Hungarians were more successful under Kossuth, who proclaimed Hungarian independence, but this lasted only a few weeks, and before long there was a new ascendancy of autocratic governments under Brandenburg in Prussia, Schwarzenburg in Austria, and Louis-Napoleon in France who in 1852 proclaimed the Second Empire. As in Palmerston's England there was a period of conservatism.

The unification of Italy began with the revolution of 1830, after which Mazzini founded the 'young Italy' movement, but real progress did not begin until the work of Cavour. Between 1858 and 1861, as a result of changing agreements with Louis-Napoleon, varying successes in war against Austria, and the contributions of Garibaldi in the south of Italy, Cavour forged a united Italy whose first parliament met in 1861. In the same year he died. In the same year also, Bismarck emerged as chief minister in Prussia and controlled Germany for the next twenty-seven years. By a similar method of negotiation, and of playing off the great powers, combined with notable military successes, Bismarck created the North German confederation in 1867, and completed the unification of Germany in 1871. The Europe of 1871 was dominated by six major powers, France, Britain, Germany, Italy, Austria-Hungary and Russia, and a new settlement had been achieved which was to last some fifty years.

What is most remarkable, however, and more interesting with regard to George Eliot, is the cultural unity of the continent. Writers and composers could move from one country to another without feeling any frontiers, and this is obvious in the lives of Lewes and George Eliot as they travel in Europe, and also appears in *Daniel Deronda* in which there is no sense created of the separateness of Europe. There is perhaps among cultured people a sense of rootlessness such as I mentioned as part of George

Eliot's preoccupation with regard to English society, and it is perhaps significant that the conclusion of *Daniel Deronda* is preoccupied with Daniel's search for a new and secure identity. This is the necessary conclusion of the outcome of *Middlemarch*. In that novel Dorothea and Ladislaw are united, but they are united in an unattached world, even though it is ultimately preferred to the world of Middlemarch with its hypocrisies and blindnesses. It is not surprising that in her next novel she should present a character similar in kind to Dorothea and to Ladislaw but looking for, and finding, a new and positively attached identity. Whether she transmutes this issue into art is a different critical matter, but it is a clear preoccupation, and one undoubtedly thrown up by the conditions of her own life, and her observations of life in Europe, especially for the intellectual during her lifetime.

4

The Novel before 1856

The novel is the hardest literary form to assess, to evaluate, or to criticise, whichever term you regard as most appropriate. Both poetry and drama are concerned with intensification. In a poem, even if it is a long one, there is, if it is good, a concentration of thought and feeling into a memorable pattern of words in which every word carries special weight. In a play, whether it is comic or tragic or any other type, there is a search for the most memorable dramatic crisis, either a comic exposure or a tragic catastrophe, and this crisis is usually identifiable as the necessary culmination of a sequence of events brought about by an interaction of characters. In both cases, unless the poem or play is unusually obscure, it is easy to decide what the writer intends, or what the work achieves, and consequently easy enough then to make a judgment.

This is not so with the novel. The novel in its nature is relatively long, in some cases very long indeed, and it is an unusual reader who sits down to read a novel straight through without stopping, and thus to gain an impression of it whole. Reading a novel is to some extent a feat of memory, unless the novel is very slight indeed. Similarly, although a novel may make use of dramatic effects and contain moments of great dramatic intensity—Tom Tulliver's discovery of Maggie and Philip in the Red Deeps, or Dorothea's breaking in on Will and Rosamund *tête-à-tête*—these are not the exclusive purpose of the novel.

What then may be the purpose of a novel—other than to entertain? It may be to present a fully rounded portrait of character, more complete and resolved than a character in a play can ever be, and yet there are many novels in which the characters are slight figures, not much more than types, and most novels only fill out a few of the central figures. It may be to present an analysis of society, either satirical or sympathetic. This is certainly true of, for instance, *Janet's Repentance* on the one hand with the picture of life in Milby, and *Middlemarch* on the other. It soon becomes clear that the novel is capable of many and diverse functions. There is perhaps only one thing that the great novels have in common and that is to tell the truth about some aspect of *human* experience. There are no novels which are not about *people*. Sometimes these are people seen exclusively as passionate individuals, sometimes seen as part of a social organisation, sometimes as both; sometimes seen objectively in relation to one overall considered view of life, as in the case of Thackeray's *Vanity Fair*; sometimes seen subjectively as extensions of the passionate inner life of the author, as in the case of Emily Brontë's *Wuthering Heights*; sometimes, in the more complex works of Jane Austen, Dickens and George Eliot, seen from a mixture of viewpoints.

The problem is equally complex when we begin to look at the formal organisation of novels, the different narrative methods and so forth, which have been very diverse even from the earliest times, setting aside the more extreme experiments in this century of James Joyce and Virginia Woolf.

The purpose of this chapter is to give some brief impression of the history of the novel up to the time when George Eliot started writing, but also to show what had been achieved in the form with regard to the ideas already mentioned. She did not make a revolutionary contribution to the form or function of the novel, but she did bring to it a greatly increased maturity. In order to show this, I have chosen to describe in slightly fuller detail four well-known novels, each of which represents a certain feature in the development of the novel form, which George Eliot was able to draw on. The four novels are *Emma* (1815), *Wuthering Heights* (1847), *Vanity Fair* (1848) and *Bleak House* (1852), bearing in mind that George Eliot started writing in 1856.

The 18th-century novel, from its earliest form in the hands of Defoe, ostensibly recounted fact, recent historical fact, for example *The Journal of the Plague Year* and *The Adventures of Robinson Crusoe*. Thus, although he is off to one side of the mainstream of the novel, Swift chose to present *Gulliver's Travels* as fact. Fielding's novels were tales of the lives of certain notorious characters, presented as fact, and Richardson's consisted of the allegedly factual letters exchanged between the characters. The novel told of real things that happened. This same technique was taken up by writers of historical fiction, such as Scott, who although he was not reporting recent and confirmable fact nevertheless based his writings on known factual occurrences. The main attitude is to some extent proved by the one form of novel which was very obviously not fact, the Gothic novel, or horror story. In this case the writer departed as far as possible from what was factually likely to have occurred, though of course the stories were still told as if they had happened.

The function of all these forms of novel in the 18th and early 19th centuries was largely to entertain and only a little to instruct. They also have no more than a loose framework when compared with the 19th-century novel.

'Emma' (1815)

The first major exponent of a tightly organised form in the novel was Jane Austen, and *Emma* remains one of the most closely organised works of art of its kind. Jane Austen portrays in her novels exclusively the part of society which she knew well, and she did this because only then could she describe what was true. Her scope is therefore narrow, and has a decidedly feminine viewpoint. Her menfolk do not engage in business, except very remotely, and the world of public life never comes nearer than vague mention of distant affairs. This does not mean, however, that her *achievement* is either narrow or superficial, because what she knew, she also understood, and had the ability to re-create not only so as to make it real, but also to interpret it with a clarity that is hardly rivalled.

The main theme of *Emma* is the development of the central character, Emma Woodhouse, of whom Jane Austen says on the first page of the novel:

> The real evils, indeed, of Emma's situation were the power of having rather too much her own way, and a disposition to think a little too well of herself.

After the marriage of her governess and confidante, Emma befriends a younger girl, Harriet Smith, of unknown parentage, from a local girls' boarding-school. Emma gives Harriet somewhat grandiose ideas of herself and of her marital expectations, and attempts to make a match between Harriet and the local vicar, Mr. Elton, which rebounds badly on her when she discovers that Elton really aspires to *her* hand, not Harriet's. What, however, is good enough for Harriet is not good enough for Emma herself, and Elton is sent packing. Emma later thinks herself in love with her former governess's stepson, Frank Churchill, and is again discomfited to discover that he is already secretly engaged. Her final and most ironical mortification arrives when she learns that Harriet has fallen in love with Mr. Knightley, Emma's lifelong friend, and the most important landowner in the district, and, what is more, believes herself encouraged by Knightley himself. Emma is at last shocked into a realisation that she is in danger of losing the only man she could love, and losing him through her vanity in patronising Harriet, and in failing to understand correctly both her own and almost everyone else's true feelings. Her distress is genuine and most lucidly exposed by Jane Austen, who only afterwards allows the right course to work its way out towards the conventional happy ending for all the major characters. Besides the irony of Emma's near loss of Knightley to Harriet, another irony arises from the arrival of the woman the rejected Elton marries, who is outstandingly objectionable both in general terms and especially to Emma whom she displaces as first lady of the small town in which they live.

All the characters in the novel are to some extent judged according to an understood principle of right conduct, which involves regard for others, especially if related, and respect for the given social order, and a rejection of selfish or egotistic motives.

It is quite clear that the link between Jane Austen and George Eliot is very strong indeed. Jane Austen is much less grand, for the most part much less serious, and has a lighter style, the humour of which is sharper and swifter. But both share the same regard for right conduct, the same rejection of any sort of egotism, the same identification of egotism in even apparently altruistic persons, the same consciousness of the complexities and perplexities of the inner life of the individual, and above all the same regard for expressing the truth of what they observe.

What Jane Austen *lacked*, though the word is scarcely appropriate, is the power to express the stronger emotions so that their strength is realised by the reader. This came most notably from another woman who like George Eliot published her work under a masculine pseudonym. *Wuthering Heights* is still unequalled in the English novel in its expression of violent passion, and Heathcliff is one of the most memorable literary creations.

'Wuthering Heights' (1847)

The particular greatness of *Wuthering Heights* lies in Emily Brontë's power to recreate the passionate nature of especially Catherine Earnshaw and Heathcliff. The events of the novel are in a sense melodramatic, but they do not read as melodrama, because the tempers of Catherine and Heathcliff are real tempers, as is the intensity of the bond between them. This is revealed at many moments in the novel, especially for example when Heathcliff visits Cathy on her death-bed; but a less intense moment and one more easily read outside its context comes when Cathy tells Nelly of her intention to marry Edgar Linton, against all her deepest instincts. While she is speaking Heathcliff is in fact listening, unknown to her.

> 'If I were in heaven, Nelly, I should be extremely miserable.'
> 'Because you are not fit to go there,' I answered. 'All sinners would be miserable in heaven.'
> 'But it is not for that. I dreamt once that I was there.'

'I tell you I won't hearken to your dreams, Miss Catherine! I'll go to bed,' I interrupted again.

She laughed, and held me down; for I made a motion to leave my chair.

'This is nothing,' cried she: 'I was only going to say that heaven did not seem to be my home; and I broke my heart with weeping to come back to earth; and the angels were so angry that they flung me out into the middle of the heath on the top of Wuthering Heights; where I woke sobbing for joy. That will do to explain my secret, as well as the other. I've no more business to be marrying Edgar Linton than I have to be in heaven; and if the wicked man in there had not brought Heathcliff so low, I shouldn't have thought of it. It would degrade me to marry Heathcliff now; so he shall never know how I love him: and that, not because he's handsome, Nelly, but because he's more myself than I am. Whatever our souls are made of, his and mine are the same; and Linton's is as different as a moonbeam from lightning, or frost from fire.'

Ere this speech had ended, I became sensible of Heathcliff's presence. Having noticed a slight movement, I turned my head, and saw him rise from the bench and steal out noiselessly. He had listened till he heard Catherine say it would degrade her to marry him, and then he stayed to hear no further.   Ch. 9

Catherine later goes on to explain how she conceives that in marrying Linton she will not desert Heathcliff, although her imaginings are now in vain. Heathcliff's already established resentment towards everything that had conspired to prevent the fulfilment of his love for Catherine is now confirmed, and the rest of the novel works it out. There are two worlds in the novel: the world called real which is the same as that which Jane Austen re-creates, and which is the world in which Edgar Linton lives, and which Cathy turns to, the world in which moral judgment is relevant; and the world called unreal, which was much more real to Emily Brontë, and is the world in which Catherine's and Heathcliff's passion would be fulfilled without ever needing to be recognised, a world in which emotion connects directly to emotion. These two worlds make a problem for the critic of *Wuthering Heights*, though few would deny its power to move the reader, or the 'reality' of the passions, but, as Jane Austen's world is in one way specialised, so is Emily Brontë's. Both express truth, the first within a known and accepted framework of moral ideas, the second according to something which scarcely acknowledges the relevance of moral ideas at all. Heathcliff's behaviour by the standards of Jane Austen's world would characterise him as a lunatic, by any *standards* as such would be called bad, even if excusable, but by the ways of life of Emily Brontë's world it is inevitable and human and therefore right, however it be judged.

Emily Brontë was writing only ten years before George Eliot began her first fiction, and there is much less connection between them as writers, except that George Eliot undoubtedly recognised as well as she the validity of human passion. Her characters are often driven by profound emotions in a way that Jane Austen's are not, but for her such passions are the root of tragedy —for Mrs. Transome in *Felix Holt*, and for Gwendolen Harleth in *Daniel Deronda*—which is not relieved by any such understood or implied post-mortal relief such as is suggested for Cathy and Heathcliff.

The other most interesting quality of *Wuthering Heights* as far as the development of the novel form is concerned is the method of narration. At no point is the reader ever conscious of the author of the book at all. The whole story is totally objectified. It is told first by Lockwood, who is a stranger to the district and to all the events of the past. He encounters Heathcliff and the household of 1801, and then learns the past history of the two families, Earnshaw and Linton, from his housekeeper, Nelly Dean. She as a simple country character offers little by way of commentary on the events of the story, and Lockwood scarcely can because he is a stranger. What he does say is soon seen to be somewhat affected, and is never built into any sort of commentary on the events. Such incidents as Nelly could not know are related either by letter or at second hand. There is a letter from Isabella Linton, describing the circumstances of her marriage to Heathcliff, and Nelly recounts some of the story as it was told her by Catherine Linton, or by Zillah, the housekeeper at Wuthering Heights. The consequences of this method are that

59

all the characters speak for themselves, and nothing is described except action and occasionally atmosphere. Even the characters are only briefly pictured, although so strongly that no further detail would be required. It is this method of narration which chiefly gives solidity to what would otherwise read as a fantastic story, closely akin to the Gothic novels. The simple personality of Nelly Dean, however, allows the reader, indeed persuades him, to suspend his disbelief quite easily. In this achievement, Emily Brontë again differs from George Eliot, who is continuously and deliberately present in her novels and who provides a continuous commentary on characters and events. Emily Brontë convinces the reader of the truth of experience in her novel, and does not need to justify Heathcliff's behaviour by her own words. Here again it is through Nelly that this is best achieved, for even towards the end, Heathcliff can still speak to Nelly out of his better nature which now has very little to call it out in the world around him. George Eliot's method is quite different from this, and some critics have preferred the type of novel which speaks for itself as *Wuthering Heights* does, and which does not need a commentary from the author. It is, however, important to observe that there is no necessary reason why one method should be better than the other. The final judgment must rest in what is achieved in each individual novel.

Vanity Fair' (1848)

A year after Emily Brontë published *Wuthering Heights*, Thackeray published *Vanity Fair* which introduced another dimension into the form of the novel, or rather confirmed in a great work what had been promised by many earlier novels. This was the great panoramic view of a society in action; not just a piece of reportage such as many 18th-century novels had been, but an organised work of satire, written deliberately as a novel without a hero and also in fact without a heroine, since although Becky Sharp attracts to herself the chief narrative interest, her character is not such as to engage the reader in her fortunes in the same way as Emma or Heathcliff does, even though both have failings. Her end, 'not with a bang but a whimper', when she affects the title of Lady Crawley to which she is not entitled and 'hangs about' Bath and Cheltenham, totally disperses any faint inclination the reader may have had to regard her as a heroine. The satire is exceedingly savage too, and is in no way deflected or softened by the traditional satiric technique of allegory. 'Vanity Fair' may be an allegorical title, but the place is England and the people are real. Sir Pitt Crawley's proposal to Becky is absurdly grotesque, but softened by being exceedingly funny. Later in the novel when his death is near, there is no humour to soften the blow:

> Of sunshiny days this old gentleman was taken out in a chair on the terrace—the very chair which Miss Crawley had had at Brighton, and which had been transported thence with a number of Lady Southdown's effects to Queen's Crawley. Lady Jane always walked by the old man; and was an evident favourite with him. He used to nod many times to her and smile when she came in, and utter inarticulate deprecatory moans when she was going away. When the door shut upon her he would cry and sob—whereupon Hester's face and manner, which was always exceedingly bland and gentle while her lady was present, would change at once, and she would make faces at him and clench her fist, and scream out, 'Hold your tongue, you stoopid old fool,' and twirl away his chair from the fire which he loved to look at—at which he would cry more. For this was all that was left after more than seventy years of cunning and struggling, and drinking, and scheming, and sin and selfishness —a whimpering old idiot put in and out of bed and cleaned and fed like a baby.   Ch. 40

Neither the idea nor the sentiment is new, but the swiftness of the blow and of the many others like it sets this novel apart, although it is not without passages where the control is less sharp.

What George Eliot had from Thackeray is probably the omniscient and remote viewpoint, although in her case any satire she offers is always tempered with compassion. Thackeray would have been much more savage towards characters like Featherstone and Brooke and Bulstrode in *Middlemarch*, and much less sympathetic towards Dorothea or Lydgate. He eyed society with a sardonic eye and saw apparently little reason to forgive its members for their follies, whereas George Eliot's sympathy is seldom far away. Even when she is most critical, she presents the situation so that it is clear how the character got into such a predicament, and it is also clear that he or she is not wholly to blame. It is this overt and continuous consciousness of the interrelationship between the life of the individual and the life of society which is George Eliot's greatest achievement.

'Bleak House' (1852)

In 1852 Dickens published *Bleak House*. The most important contribution that Dickens made to the form of the novel as far as we are concerned at present is in the construction of elaborate and involved plots. *Bleak House* is a long and complex novel with many more important features than the ramifications of its plot, but it serves as a useful example of the control required to keep in hand several threads of a unified plot amid a vast amount of incident and characterisation and with the additional complication of a double narrative.

Unlike *Wuthering Heights*, where the narrative is told by several individuals as a natural consequence of the situation, in *Bleak House* Dickens creates a wholly artificial effect. The story is shared between the impersonal narrator, understood to be Dickens (but given no identity except that which arises anyway from style and tone) and Esther Summerson, who is a character in the other narrative. The effect of this is to provide the limited viewpoint of Esther contrasted with the viewpoint of the impersonal narrator who knows much more than Esther knows. It also permits Dickens a greater range of character portrayal, especially as Esther is for the most part totally sympathetic with the characters she meets, whereas the other narrator is much more continuously critical. The interweaving of the two narratives provides valuable opportunities for suspense, since at several key moments Dickens leaves Esther and takes up the story himself, or vice versa.

However, this technical experiment, which is not wholly

successful because so patently contrived, is not the most important formal feature of the novel. The extremely involved plot is more important because it is integrated with a complete poetic image which dominates every part of the whole work and contributes more than anything else to its unification. The range and purpose of the plot is pointed out by Dickens himself in the course of the novel.

> What connexion can there be between the place in Lincolnshire, the house in town, the Mercury in powder, and the whereabout of Jo the outlaw with the broom, who had that distant ray of light upon him when he swept the churchyard step? What connexion can there have been between many people in the innumerable histories of this world who from opposite sides of great gulfs have nevertheless been very curiously brought together? Ch. 16

Lady Dedlock lives in 'the place in Lincolnshire' and keeps the town house and the powdered servant. Jo is a London street-boy who sweeps the road-crossings, and who in total contrast with Lady Dedlock is the lowest representative of humanity in the novel, and it is clear that part of the whole conception arises from Dickens's fascination with this type of link and contrast. This is by no means the only one, though it is the most distant and unlikely. More than half the novel is concerned with the gradual unravelling of the events which have brought about the connection between Jo and Lady Dedlock—her past life, and her love of Captain Hawdon, who when also down-and-out befriends Jo, slowly teased out of minute clues by her husband's sinister solicitor, Mr. Tulkinghorn, and the mystery surrounding Esther, who proves to be Lady Dedlock's daughter. When this has been made clear, the novel then hinges on whether Lady Dedlock will be exposed, which matter culminates in the murder of Mr. Tulkinghorn at a point when he is just about to expose her. Lady Dedlock is not responsible, but the shame of the revelation drives her from her home to her eventual death from exposure at the graveside of her lover who had died much earlier in the book.

As sketchy a summary as that serves to show what type of

story it is, and it must also be said that the story, like the narrative method, creaks a good deal, so concerned is Dickens to bring into play the whole gamut of social types in all classes and in as many modes of employment as possible. But the plot is not the only unifying force. More successful is the use of the High Court of Chancery and the case of Jarndyce and Jarndyce to which in some way or other every character is a party, if not as a direct suitor then by some consequence arising out of a suit, or some connection with a suitor. Chancery and the processes of law are given a rapid identity at the outset of the novel when Dickens describes a London fog, and

> hard by Temple Bar, in Lincoln's Inn Hall, at the very heart of the fog, sits the Lord High Chancellor in his High Court of Chancery.
> Ch. I

and beyond this too is another set of images which act as a much more savage and ultimately more memorable unifying force in the novel. These are the images of disease, grief and death. It is not a happy novel, despite its happy ending. Death is frequent in it, arising both from disease and neglect. A baby dies very early on, chiefly from neglect; Hawdon dies of an overdose of opium; Krook dies, astonishingly, from spontaneous combustion, giving rise to one of the most extraordinary ghoulish passages of description in any novel, as the inhabitants of the area where Krook lives become aware of the strange smell as of the cooking of bad meat, the flakes of greasy soot in the air, and the patches of oil on the window-sills; Jo dies of neglect and exposure; Lady Dedlock dies of grief and exposure; Gridley dies of exhaustion following his involvement with the Chancery suit which has sapped his life; and he is later followed by Richard Carstone, one of the wards in Chancery, who is also worn away by the lawsuit. All these die as a consequence in one way or another of the grasping tentacles of the law and lawyers. Even Esther to whom is given a happy conclusion is struck down by small-pox and permanently disfigured because she tries to help Jo when he is also diseased, and it is clearly relevant that the only 'straight' character in the book, the only one who is not deformed, is the surgeon Allen Woodcourt, who for the most part is away from England and the corruption, and when he returns helps to alleviate it. Notable deformities in connection with the law are Mr. Vholes who is completely a parasite on the law, and whose only interest is to suck his welfare out of the law's victims, and the much more fundamentally sinister Mr. Tulkinghorn, whose relentless search for the truth of Lady Dedlock's history is the cause of her downfall. Both of these men are in their whole presentation cold and chill and frighteningly unhuman. The novel is full of other characters with various distortions and deformities of body and character: Mr. Smallfield, paralysed from the waist down, and beset with greed; Mr. Skimpole, grotesquely and revoltingly irresponsible about money, having invented a perverted justification of his irresponsibility in his alleged incapability of understanding anything about money at all. This character incidentally appears almost entirely in the angelic Esther's narrative, and is consequently presented always with sympathy, which makes his affected naïvety even more repellent.

The novel deals savagely with many forms of abuse both personal and social. It attacks the law chiefly: 'The one great principle of the English law is to make business for itself'; but also poverty and the slums, and the fecklessness of do-gooders who turn their attentions to Borioboola-Gha, while neglecting not only the needs around them in a general way, but also the particular needs of their families. But, as a buttress against these vices, it offers only the solace of the world to come, 'the world that sets this right', the casual relief of compassion, though this compassion does not always succeed, the romanticised possibilities of philanthropy, expressed through John Jarndyce but not really made alive, and finally the sound practical sense of men like Inspector Bucket. Dickens offers very little else. He does not offer a stringent moral pattern as a means of escape from the horror, nor does he look to the possibility of either social or political reform. For both of these, in various ways, the novel waited for George Eliot.

The purpose of this chapter has been to show some of the possibilities of the form of the novel, and to show by contrast what George Eliot might have learnt, either to use or reject, from her predecessors. Each of the four novels discussed achieves something special in its own right, and Emily Brontë and Charles Dickens created works of art of an originality that makes them stand out now. George Eliot did not so successfully create scenes of intense passion such as are in *Wuthering Heights*, nor did she ever construct such powerful poetic images as Dickens, who achieved this not only in *Bleak House*, but also and equally compellingly through the prison imagery in *Little Dorrit*, and the river Thames in *Our Mutual Friend*. She did, however, contribute through one of her most deeply held convictions something to the novel which none of her predecessors had achieved—a sense of the absolute reality of the lives of almost all her characters.

5

The Old World

All George Eliot's novels before and including *Romola* may be seen as works in which she learnt how to overcome problems of characterisation, plot, description, choice of incident, emphasis and so forth. At the same time, apart from *Scenes of Clerical Life*, they are not apprentice works. Some aspects of *Adam Bede*, *The Mill on the Floss*, and *Romola* itself are as great as anything she later achieved, but these books are also flawed in such a damaging way that they do not relate as works of art to *Felix Holt* which marks the turning point, or more especially to *Middlemarch* and *Daniel Deronda*. The main reasons for this difference lie in George Eliot's powers of characterisation and in her control of the story. In *Adam Bede*, Adam himself and Dinah Morris are endowed with heroic qualities which ultimately diminish their power as characters in art, although they are both perhaps more compelling to the popular imagination, or certainly were then. And the situations such as Hetty Sorrel's reprieve, and the glamourised picture of Arthur Donnithorne—even his name is Arthur—add to the romantic elements in the novel. In *The Mill on the Floss*, although the characterisation is much advanced, Stephen Guest is still an incompletely realised 'hero' and the story is made very difficult to take by the melodramatic and tear-jerking conclusion. The problems in *Romola* are different, although here too Romola herself is exalted while Baldassarre is made excessively melodramatic.

This leads us to the difficult problem of taste, and the question how should we judge qualities in a novel which are undoubtedly consequences of contemporary taste. The answer is simple enough if we relate the problem to Shakespeare. Two outstanding qualities of Shakespeare's plays are undoubtedly a consequence of Elizabethan taste; the number of corpses, and the number of puns. Both of these are in many instances excessive to modern taste, but we do not make such heavy weather of this as we do of the question of sentimentality in the Victorian novel. In the case for example of *Hamlet*, the number of deaths is a necessary dramatic consequence of the curse which hangs over Hamlet and the state of Denmark, and is presented in a manner that is dramatically decorous. Much the same can be said of Hamlet's word-play during his assumed madness. The dramatic function and necessity of each is made clear in relation to the whole work of art and therefore acceptable, in a way that the same features are not in, say, *Titus Andronicus*, or some of the early comedies.

The death then of Milly Barton in the first *Scene* is not made significant enough within the whole framework of the story to survive the charge of sentimentality, nor are the death of Wybrow, and Tina's subsequent ravings, significant enough to survive the charge of melodrama, and it is doubtful whether the wholly tear-jerking or spine-chilling scene ever can be, although, within the much more tightly organised and controlled *Silas Marner*, the sentimental occasion of Eppie preferring to stay with her foster-father rather than to go to her real father does not repel the reader; it is inevitable, given the moral framework of the whole book.

Ultimately there must remain a problem here which is only resolved subjectively by the reader. In *Bleak House*, there are many incidents charged with sentiment, notably for example the death of Jo the crossing-sweeper, who is encouraged to speak the opening phrases of the Lord's Prayer before he dies, and it is obvious that the whole episode evokes from Dickens the fullest expression of his compassionate horror at such examples of poverty and neglect. The passage is highly important within the framework of *Bleak House* and it is given significance, but it is still too sentimental for many modern readers.

There is, apart from the death of Milly Barton, a number of instances of sentimentality in the early novels of George Eliot, especially for instance the long-awaited arrival of Dinah Morris to console Hetty in prison. This is heralded by Dinah's own words which in any other context would seem startling:

'Can I get into the prison, if you please?' Ch. 45

In the story, this moment and what follows are charged with the sort of emotion which was most to the Victorian taste. Lewes and George Eliot used to cry over the novels they read together, and one does not need to say any more than that. The chapter is sentimentally affecting; but these opening words of Dinah force on the reader something beyond the emotion, and something which is part of the structure of the novel. Hetty is in prison, not only because she has murdered her own child. She is imprisoned in the limitations of her own personality, her self-indulgent womanliness, and her present plight is a consequence of this. Dinah is in these terms free. She can act as she will in the world because she has understood the heavy responsibilities which freedom of action involves. Her respect for duty frees her of the shackles of selfishness which have dragged Hetty down, although George Eliot is careful to maintain the reader's sympathy for Hetty. In this way, the sentimental effect of the chapter (45) is controlled by its function in the shape of the novel. Another criticism can be made, which is that the symbolic pattern is rather too obvious, and this is probably a fair criticism, but one that belongs with the overall criticism of this novel, in which both Adam himself and Dinah are treated more romantically than was characteristic in the later work.

'SCENES OF CLERICAL LIFE'

These three stories are not now much read though they merit reading more than most of the minor works of great writers. In relation to other prose works of the period they are short indeed, although the third of them, *Janet's Repentance*, is as long as a good many novels published in this century, and fully as rich in content. However, in relation to the later novels they are only interesting in showing the general trend and tone of George Eliot's imagination. Their flaws consist chiefly of a lack of control of style, and an inadequate balance between the possible scope and depth of the stories and their characters and what she actually achieved.

This latter detail applies less in the case of *Amos Barton*, which is a slight enough story and does not strain the framework she chose for it. Its main quality is the very ordinariness of the characters and the situations, pointed up by the narrator, who is understood to be a man, though he is not given any significant character.

> Depend upon it, you would gain unspeakably if you would learn with me to see some of the poetry and the pathos, the tragedy and the comedy, lying in the experience of a human soul that looks out through dull grey eyes, and speaks in a voice of quite ordinary tones. In that case, I should have no fear of your not caring to know what farther befell the Rev. Amos Barton, or of your thinking the homely details I have to tell at all beneath your attention. As it is, you can, if you please, decline to pursue my story farther; and you will easily find reading more to your taste, since I learn from the newspapers that many remarkable novels full of striking situations, thrilling incidents, and eloquent writing, have appeared only within the last season.
>
> Ch. 5

This is all rather disingenuous, because George Eliot, even as early as this, does not shy away from 'eloquence' and both the stories which she was already working on when this was published have in them striking situations, and if not positively thrilling, then certainly melodramatic ingredients. In other words, this is a rhetorical device to draw the reader's attention to the importance of sympathising with people who live little lives such as are described in the story. Nevertheless it is an extremely important part of George Eliot's total vision. The 'dull, grey eyes', and 'the voice of quite ordinary tones' are always very important to her, and in all the later novels there are people who are ordinary, but who as a result of her special sympathy and insight are given what of course they always had, their own individuality. Hetty Sorrel in *Adam Bede* is an ordinary girl whose ordinariness gets her into the extraordinary plight of murdering her unwanted child. She is, for example, much more ordinary than Tess

Durbeyfield, whose situation is somewhat similar, but who is always set apart. Silas Marner is ordinary, and so are the Rev. Rufus Lyon in *Felix Holt* and many of the characters in *Middlemarch*, though by this time George Eliot had the power to create and control characters and incidents which were not merely ordinary. Dorothea is no ordinary woman, but the world she lives in is, and that is part of her problem. It is striking then that George Eliot's first work of fiction should be so strongly orientated to ordinary people with 'dull, grey eyes' and 'voices of quite ordinary tones'. Actually no later work of hers so completely relied on that kind of character in that kind of setting, but she had as it were set a standpoint from which she never deviated, which was that she would write truthfully about real people.

The style of the passage quoted above shows how uneasy George Eliot was at this stage. It is highly self-conscious, and it is getting at the reader, which she does even more off-puttingly earlier in the story:

> Reader! *did* you ever taste such a cup of tea as Miss Gibbs is this moment handing to Mr. Pilgrim? Do you know the dulcet strength, the animating blandness of tea sufficiently blended with real farmhouse cream? No—most likely you are a miserable town-bred reader, who think of cream as a thinnish white fluid, delivered in infinitesimal pennyworths down area steps; or perhaps from a presentiment of calves' brains, you refrain from any lacteal addition, and rasp your tongue with unmitigated bohea.   Ch. 1

The sheer vocabulary of this passage and the concentration of it is disturbing, but when one observes that it concerns the quality of cream and whether or not one takes it in tea, there is an obvious disproportion of tone and subject.

But the short novel already has the sharp penetration which is characteristic of George Eliot both in her early and her mature works. Very soon after the lines just quoted, she describes Mrs. Patten in a way that makes you wonder how her judgment could have erred in the earlier piece. She has just described Mrs. Hackit and her incessant knitting:

> Mrs. Patten does not admire this excessive click-clicking activity. Quiescence in an easy-chair, under the sense of compound interest perpetually accumulating, has long seemed an ample function for her and she does her malevolence gently. She is a pretty little old woman of eighty, with a close cap and and tiny flat white curls round her face, as natty and unsoiled and invariable as the waxen image of a little old lady under a glass-case; once a lady's-maid, and married for her beauty. She used to adore her husband, and now she adores her money, cherishing a quiet blood-relation's hatred for her niece, Janet Gibbs, who, she knows, expects a large legacy, and whom she is determined to disappoint. Her money shall all go in a lump to a distant relation of her husband's, and Janet shall be saved the trouble of pretending to cry, by finding that she has been left a miserable pittance. Ch. 1

Here the concentration is in the observation and the satire. The style is altogether tightened up, and the balance of terse phrases carries the force of the characterisation.

The same sharp assessments are used when George Eliot describes the Countess Czerlaski and Amos himself. The 'Countess', whom local people have invested with a reputation of glamorous mystery, was a governess who married a Polish dancing-master, now dead, and who had settled in Milby because she could better compete there than in a more fashionable spot. George Eliot's comment again shows the sharper style which she already could achieve and in this instance she uses it to express much more acutely her concentration on the ordinariness of people. She has just told the real story of the Countess.

> All this, which was the simple truth, would have seemed extremely flat to the gossips of Milby, who had made up their minds to something much more exciting. There was nothing here so very detestable. It is true, the Countess was a little vain, a little ambitious, a little selfish, a little shallow and frivolous, a little given to white lies. But who considers such slight blemishes, such moral pimples as these, disqualifications for entering into the most respectable society! Indeed, the severest ladies in Milby would have been perfectly aware that these characteristics would have created no wide distinction between the Countess Czerlaski and themselves. Ch. 4

Chapter I.

In the days when the spinning-wheels hummed busily in the farm-houses, & even great ladies, clothed in silk & thread lace, had their toy spinning-wheels of mahogany or polished oak, there might be seen, in districts far away among the lanes or deep in the bosom of the hills, certain pallid undersized men, who, by the side of the brawny country folk, looked like the remnants of a disinherited race. The shepherd's dog barked fiercely when one of these alien-looking men appeared on the upland, dark against the early winter sunset; for what dog likes a figure bent under a heavy bag? — & these pale men rarely stirred abroad without that mysterious burthen. The shepherd himself, though he had good reason to believe that the bag held nothing but flaxen thread or else the long rolls of strong linen spun from that thread, was not quite sure that this trade of weaving, indispensable though it was, could be carried on entirely without the help of the evil one. In that far-off time superstition clung easily round every person or thing that was at all unwonted, or even intermittent & occasional merely, like the visits of the pedlar or the knife-grinder. No one knew where wandering men had their homes or

The election of 1857. From an engraving by Phiz.

The 1850 portrait of George Eliot, by Durade.

Arbury Hall. George Eliot frequently wrote at the stone table in the foreground.

The same idea emerges when she describes Amos as well:

> And, after all, the Rev. Amos never came near the borders of a vice. His very faults were middling—he was not *very* ungrammatical. It was not in his nature to be superlative in anything; unless indeed he was superlatively middling.

Milly Barton is idealised in a way that produces another imbalance in a story which contains such a clear and sharp portrait both of Amos and of the society of Milby, and her death which has been briefly discussed above is a much less successful part of the tale. It gives rise, however, to one of the most important themes of all George Eliot's work, the importance of human sympathy and the tragic reality of its fading. Three short passages serve to illustrate this theme, and all three of them also show the comparative unsureness of George Eliot's style at this early stage. Milly has died and been buried:

> It was Mr. Cleves who buried her. On the first news of Mr. Barton's calamity, he had ridden over from Tripplegate to beg that he might be made of some use, and his silent grasp of Amos's hand had penetrated like the painful thrill of life-recovering warmth to the poor benumbed heart of the stricken man. Ch. 9

> Amos Barton had been an affectionate husband, and while Milly was with him, he was never visited by the thought that perhaps his sympathy with her was not quick and watchful enough; but now he re-lived all their life together, with that terrible keenness of memory and imagination which bereavement gives, and he felt as if his very love needed a pardon for its poverty and selfishness. Ch. 9

And then some time later, after he has been moved to another living, when he visits Milly's grave just before leaving:

> He stood for a few minutes reading over and over again the words on the tombstone, as if to assure himself that all the happy and unhappy past was a reality. For love is frightened at the intervals of insensibility and callousness that encroach little by little on the dominion of grief, and it makes efforts to recall the keenness of the first anguish. Ch. 10

Each of these passages shows clearly the tendency of George Eliot's main preoccupations, and both the subsequent stories develop this theme further. In *Mr. Gilfil's Love-Story* it is Maynard Gilfil's continuing affection for Tina, who does not return it until it is too late, that is seen as a redemptive power, and this is enlarged even further and much more clearly in the case of *Janet's Repentance*, where Janet is positively saved by the sympathy of the Rev. Edgar Tryan.

Mr. Gilfil's Love-Story is a more substantial creation than *Amos Barton*. In it, George Eliot widens her range of characters considerably, in particular to take in the aristocratic family of Sir Christopher Cheveril, and to develop a much more ambitious plot involving a romantic love affair. While various features of the novel mark a great advance, it is generally regarded as the least successful of George Eliot's prose works, with the exception of the short story, *Brother Jacob*. The main reason for this is the unrelieved sense of melodrama that accompanies the death of Sir Christopher's nephew, Anthony Wybrow. Sir Christopher has adopted an orphaned Italian girl, Tina, who is violently in love with Wybrow, and has in the past received some indication that her love is returned, although the reader knows that Wybrow is selfish and superficial and that Tina is misled. When events reach a crisis after Wybrow's betrothed tells Tina that she is totally mistaken if she believes Wybrow has ever given her cause to hope, Tina rushes to a cabinet of weapons in the house and takes a dagger with intent to kill Wybrow. She does not do so, because on reaching the Rookery where she knows he will be, she finds him already dead of a heart attack. The melodrama then is never actually realised, except in the passionate Tina's imagination, but the tone of melodrama through the relevant chapters is uncontrolled, even to the extent of moving into the present tense to heighten the immediacy of the events, and there is no redeeming irony whatsoever.

> Good God! it is he—lying motionless—his hat fallen. He is ill, then—he has fainted. Her hand lets go the dagger, and she rushes towards him. His eyes are fixed; he does not see her. She sinks down

on her knees, takes the dear dead head in her arms, and kisses the cold forehead.

'Anthony, Anthony! speak to me—it is Tina—speak to me! O God, he is dead!'

Ch. 13

This must seem comic to all but the most naïve taste, although it did not apparently have such an effect in its own day. However, there are other features of the story which are very important indeed with regard to the later novels. Wybrow's self-indulgent flirting with Tina clearly grows into the more subtle relationship between Arthur Donnithorne and Hetty Sorrel in *Adam Bede*. Wybrow is George Eliot's first attempt at the portrayal of characters whose egotism is combined with charm and who are not in any way set apart from their surroundings because of their selfishness, unlike the Countess Czerlaski, who is from the start rather false and rather unlikeable. Wybrow is decent enough at first, and Arthur Donnithorne certainly is. George Eliot is also continuously interested in the contrasts of affection that arise when parental relationships are complicated by adoptions and so forth. Sir Christopher looks on Wybrow as his heir, but retains a strong affection for his ward, Maynard Gilfil, who has been brought up with Tina and who loves her truly in a way Wybrow could hardly comprehend. This is a pattern which, much altered, re-emerges in *Daniel Deronda* with Sir Hugo Mallinger, whose heir is Henleigh Grandcourt, but whose strongest affection goes to his ward, Daniel Deronda. Both young men also are, in much more complex ways than in this story, involved with the same woman, Gwendolen Harleth. The atmosphere of this short novel is also similar to that of *Daniel Deronda*, and like nothing in between, even though aristocratic families do figure in *Felix Holt* and in *Middlemarch*. There are descriptive passages of scenery which although effective are a little uncharacteristic:

the castellated house of grey-tinted stone, with the flickering sun-beams sending dashes of golden light across the many-shaped panes in the mullioned windows, and a great beech leaning athwart one of the flanking towers, and breaking, with its dark flattened boughs,

75

the too formal symmetry of the front: the broad gravel-walk winding on the right, by a row of tall pines, alongside the pool—on the left branching out among swelling grassy mounds, surmounted by clumps of trees, where the red trunk of the Scotch fir glows in the descending sunlight against the bright green of the limes and acacias. . . .

Ch. 2

The passage continues in this vogue and shows what fine talent George Eliot had for landscape painting. It is not in any way a purple passage, or in its context even a set-piece. Every detail speaks for itself, leaving the reader in the scene without being asked to observe any significance except what it is. This power of description is one of George Eliot's least-noted gifts, and it reappears outstandingly in *Daniel Deronda*.

Finally, in connection with *Mr. Gilfil's Love-Story*, there is the same theme of human sympathy as a redeeming power. After the death of Wybrow, Tina flees from Cheverel Manor and is totally overcome with a sense of her own guilt, even though she did not commit the murder (another theme, incidentally, which re-emerges in *Daniel Deronda*). Maynard finds her, and restores her to some degree of health and marries her, though she is too much weakened to live long after that. He helps her in this restoration sheerly by listening sympathetically so that she, in terms of modern psychology, can externalise her emotional tensions.

In this way—in these broken confessions and answering words of comfort, the hours wore on, from the deep black night to the chill early twilight, and from early twilight to the first yellow streak of morning parting the purple cloud. Mr. Gilfil felt as if in the long hours of that night the bond that united his love for ever and alone to Caterina had acquired fresh strength and sanctity. It is so with the human relations that rest on the deep emotional sympathy of affection: every new day and night of joy and sorrow is a new ground, a new consecration, for the love that is nourished by memories as well as hopes—the love to which perpetual repetition is not a weariness but a want, and to which a separate joy is the beginning of pain.

Ch. 19

Gilfil, too, brings comfort to Sir Christopher who is broken down by the death of Wybrow on whom he had looked for the continuation of his family, since he had no son.

> At last the Baronet mastered himself enough to say:
> 'I'm very weak, Maynard—God help me! I didn't think any-thing would unman me in this way; but I'd built everything on that lad. Perhaps I've been wrong in not forgiving my sister. She lost one of *her* sons a little while ago. I've been too proud and obstinate.'
> 'We can hardly learn humility and tenderness enough except by suffering,' said Maynard.   Ch. 18

Incidents like these show how fully George Eliot's patterns of moral thought were established before she began to write, and the most striking feature of *Scenes of Clerical Life* is how far the technique falls behind the power of conception and imagination.

If *Mr. Gilfil's Love-Story* foreshadows some features of *Adam Bede* and of *Daniel Deronda*, it is *Janet's Repentance* that stands before *The Mill on the Floss, Felix Holt* and *Middlemarch*. It is in this story that George Eliot first attempts to realise the affairs of a whole community, and the story's reputation has relied a good deal on the portrait of Milby which forms Chapter Two. George Eliot opens the novel dramatically. It is in fact the only one of her novels which enters straight into a situation in this way:

> 'No!' said lawyer Dempster, in a loud rasping, oratorical tone, struggling against chronic huskiness, 'as long as my maker grants me power of voice and power of intellect, I will take every legal means to resist the introduction of demoralising, methodistical doctrine into this parish. . . .'   Ch. 1

This is one of the best openings she ever achieves, and is remark-ably modern in effect. It presents us with the objectionable Dempster very tersely, and opens the theme of the novel immediately, which is the conflict between the established society and the arrival of new doctrines of religion in the person of the Reverend Edgar Tryan. Dempster is the epitome of boorish insensitive conservatism and he arouses the town to a frenzied condition of distaste for the new preacher, concluding his efforts in a grand burlesque intended to discredit Tryan. Only a few of the townspeople support the Methodist minister, among whom is Dempster's wife Janet, whom he has always treated harshly. He is that strange and allegedly English phenomenon, a wife-beater. He is also an alcoholic, and dies a ghastly and protracted death from delirium tremens combined with meningitis. George Eliot seldom attempted anything more violent than this, and it is not a failure, though her portrait of Milby society was somewhat toned down at the request of her publisher, Blackwood. The story, as may be quickly assumed, is not, however, endearing. Dempster is very unpleasant. Janet, while greatly wronged, is not idealised, nor is Edgar Tryan. This is in some ways George Eliot's most continuously stern piece of writing. After Chapter One, in which a good deal of small-minded provincial bigotry is expressed by the characters to the accompaniment of a great deal of drinking on the part of Dempster, the author begins Chapter Two thus:

> The conversation just recorded is not, I am aware, remarkably refined or witty; but if it had been, it could hardly have taken place in Milby when Mr. Dempster flourished there, and old Mr. Crewe, the curate, was yet alive.

It is not often that novelists tell the truth like that, with no sugaring technique. Thackeray was as tough, but his whole setting invited his ferocity and it was clear to his readers that he was writing satirically. George Eliot does not write ostensible satire. She writes sympathetically and then lays on the hammer. What follows, which is presented as a *defence* of the modern Milby, is equally savage:

> More than a quarter of a century has slipped by since then, and in the interval Milby has advanced at as rapid a pace as other market-towns in her Majesty's dominions. By this time it has a handsome railway station, where the drowsy London traveller may look out by the brilliant gas-light and see perfectly sober papas and husbands alighting with their leather bags after transacting their day's business at the county town. There is a resident rector, who appeals to the consciences of his hearers with all the immense advantages

of a divine who keeps his own carriage; and the church is enlarged by at least five hundred sittings; and the grammar school conducted on reformed principles has its upper forms crowded with the genteel youth of Milby. The gentlemen there fall into no other excess at dinner parties than the perfectly well-bred and virtuous excess of stupidity; and are never known to take too much in any other way. The conversation is sometimes quite literary, for there is a flourishing book-club, and many of the younger ladies have carried their studies so far as to have forgotten a little German. In short, Milby is now a refined, moral, and enlightened town. . . . Ch. 2

When Dickens was savage, he attacked institutions, and sometimes the establishment in a generalised way; he seldom attacked the bourgeois in as savage a way as this nor as directly, and one can understand why Blackwood was as worried as he was, for he knew what George Eliot's readership would be. The whole chapter is a remarkable piece of thoroughly poker-faced satirical attack on the petty viciousness of provincial society and is not surpassed in its kind by anything that George Eliot wrote later.

'ADAM BEDE'

In immediate contrast, this novel contained much less to worry Blackwood, and its chief failings for 20th-century readers are perhaps those qualities which appealed to Victorian readers. Its most important theme is its expression of the value of a settled and rooted rural existence, and it is set at the turn of the 18th century, so that George Eliot was able to concentrate on the undisturbed rural community and to avoid all but the slightest reference to urban life. Dinah Morris's work in Stonyshire incorporates the idea of the towns into the story, but they are deliberately held at a distance.

The characters are in certain ways simplified and fitted to acceptable patterns. Adam himself is glamourised in one way, and Dinah in another. The Poyser household is kept broadly appealing and it is commonly admired even though it might have been presented as a portrait of short-sighted and self-important provincialism. The sorrows of Hetty Sorrel are not sorrows which would impinge very strongly upon George Eliot's readers, and the associated condemnation of Donnithorne is not therefore brought home to roost. It is not surprising that this novel was read with great pleasure by Queen Victoria.

I have already indicated (p. 69) the relationship between the popular elements of the story and one of the basic moral themes, that of Dinah's dedication to duty contrasted with Hetty's vain self-absorption. In general, this seems to be the best way of approaching this novel. It contains two themes which are absolutely typical of George Eliot—her belief in the importance of tradition and of a settled community, and with regard to personal life her preoccupation with self-knowledge leading to an understanding of one's duty contrasted with self-ignorance leading usually to personal tragedy. At the same time these themes are set in a story which both in action and characterisation is not typical of her.

Plot and Construction

Adam Bede is much longer than all three *Scenes of Clerical Life* taken together, and the organisation and cohesion of its plot is very remarkable when one considers George Eliot's inexperience of writing fiction up to that time. I have pointed out some of the technical exercises in the *Scenes*, but there is nothing in them which would lead one to expect the achievement of *Adam Bede* so soon after.

The novel covers the period from June 1799 to June 1807, but most of it is set between the summer of 1799 and the following spring. Only the last eight chapters take the novel on in time. George Eliot's handling of time is natural and unselfconscious. When she needs to describe a period of time in detail she does so without hesitation. The whole of Book Three, five chapters, is devoted to the single day of Arthur Donnithorne's twenty-first birthday celebrations, the Coming-of-Age of the Squire's heir and therefore a vital episode in the life of the village community. When she needs to move on in time, she does so too, always concentrating on the significant action of the significant character in relation to her themes. Chapters 32 to 35 move briskly from August 1799 to February 1801, from Arthur's departure and desertion of Hetty to Hetty's flight from Hayslope to avoid the shame of exposure over her pregnancy. George Eliot uses time in this novel as a dramatist does, selecting and focusing where her purposes demand, but she does not intend us to focus only on the drama of the story even in the climax in Book Five, and it is most important to see why she incorporates lengthy descriptions of such episodes as Dinah's first preaching on the village green, the gatherings in the Poysers' farm kitchen, Arthur's birthday celebrations, and the harvest supper at the Poysers' in Book Six. It is obvious that these are not necessary at such length to the central drama of Adam, Arthur and Hetty. They are, however, vital to the broad theme of the novel which is the importance of a rooted community life based on traditional forms and patterns. This is why George Eliot interrupts the drama at an unexpected point in Chapter 32. Hetty has just read Arthur's letter and is in a state of distress in Chapter 31. Then in Chapter 32 we apparently leave the main thread of the plot and observe an interlude in which Squire Donnithorne makes a proposal to the Poysers of an adjustment of their land. Mrs. Poyser, unable to contain herself, tells the Squire what she thinks of him, and the chapter ends with the Poysers' fears of being turned out on the following Michaelmas. Poyser's closing remark states the theme most clearly.

> '*I'm* none for worreting,' said Mr. Poyser, rising from his three-cornered chair and walking slowly towards the door; 'but I should be loth to leave th'old place, and the parish where I was bred and born, and father afore me. We should leave our roots behind us, I doubt, and niver thrive again.'   Ch. 32

The three-cornered chair and Poyser's *slow* walk are all part of the settled life he leads, and the reference to his father is another aspect of it, and it is also important to notice that this whole episode foreshadows the much more crucial one when Hetty's shame also nearly obliges the Poysers to leave. They remain on both occasions; Adam eventually takes over Burge's timber-yard and marries Dinah, who as Mrs. Poyser's niece is better to be settled in the community than carrying on her work as a Methodist in Snowfield, as far at least as the Poysers and the community are concerned. In this novel George Eliot is only concerned to show the value of the traditional village community in the support it gives to all its members, and it is this aspect of the theme which unites the broad descriptive detail with the dramatic plot. It is the stability of the community life which helps it to survive the shock imposed on it by the *unnatural* behaviour of Arthur and Hetty, and that stability is vested in such figures as Mr. Irwine, Bartle Massey the schoolmaster, and Mrs. Poyser, none of which is presented with the same romantic tinge that slightly distorts the portraits of Adam and Dinah in one way and Arthur and Hetty in another.

From the point of view of construction, it is Books One and Five which are the most interesting. The other four books are both simpler in narrative method, and more obvious in their contribution to the story.

Book One is in two parts. Chapters 1 to 11 form an introduction in which the community and its most important characters are established, and yet even this is not done either mechanically or obviously. As early as Chapter 4, we are involved with the death of Thias Bede, the type of incident which shows the community at work. The novel begins with a portrait of Adam and Seth Bede with their work-mates in Burge's workshop, establishing at first the image of a community at work. We move rapidly to Dinah's preaching on the green which gives an opportunity to enlarge on the whole community, and we can also see in this chapter George Eliot's awareness of the chance links in life, something which all the Victorian novelists had in common. The man who watches Dinah preach and sees and admires Adam proves later to be Colonel Townley, a magistrate, who is at the jail in Stoniton when Dinah arrives to see Hetty. This type of casual and not particularly meaningful link was something which the Victorian novel's expansiveness allowed with some ease. Further suggestions of the future are laid in this chapter in a more direct way when in her sermon Dinah rebukes Bessy Cranage for her vanity and her preoccupation with 'earrings and fine gowns and caps', an obvious suggestion of Hetty.

In the next few chapters we are shown the major characters in varied and interesting encounters, all of which build up the reader's sense of the community in a flexible way. From Dinah's preaching we move to Seth, and then to Adam and their mother at home, and to the death of Thias Bede, preceded by the curious episode of the sound on the door, while Adam is working through the night on the coffin his father failed to make. After this, there is a break to the Rev. Irwine, Arthur Donnithorne, and then the Poysers and Hetty. Arthur visits the Poysers and encounters Hetty, while Irwine talks to Dinah—an equally important encounter in view of their shared place in the climax, Irwine supporting Adam, and Dinah restoring Hetty to some measure of peace of mind. The final encounters, by which time the main lines of the story are laid, occur when Dinah visits Lisbeth Bede to console her after her husband's death, and while there meets Adam.

The last five chapters of Book One set the plot in motion. Arthur starts to become increasingly involved with Hetty, and the Book ends with two chapters in which Dinah and Hetty are contrasted, and then Arthur and Adam. The village setting, its main characters, and the four central characters around whom the plot revolves, are all fully established by this time.

Book Two develops the character of Adam in the context of the village, and deals with his father's funeral, his expectations with regard to the management of the Squire's woods, and his hopes with regard to Hetty. In this connection there is another theme in the book. Both Adam and Seth fall in love with the wrong woman, and it takes time and some suffering to bring their lives into order. Seth says to his mother:

> 'But, mother, thee know'st we canna love just where other folks
> 'ud have us.'   Ch. 4

Book Three is entirely given to Arthur Donnithorne's birthday party, into which is woven the constant awareness of what is developing between Arthur and Hetty, and Adam's consciousness of Hetty, and this leads quickly to the opening of Book Four in which Adam sees Arthur and Hetty kissing in the wood, and fights Arthur. This is followed by Arthur's departure and, as mentioned above, the novel moves rapidly on to Hetty's flight in February 1800. The gradual development of Adam's 'engagement' to Hetty is passed over slightly, since it is both predictable and falsely based as the reader knows well, and George Eliot is anxious to move on to more important things.

It is Book Five that really shows what a broad command George Eliot already had of the constructional problems of a long novel. All the most important dramatic episodes occur in this Book and all the major characters experience some sort of crisis. The Book falls into three parts, but these are neither equal in length nor exactly consecutive. The first strand is Hetty's story, the second Adam's and the third Arthur's, with Mr. Irwine and Dinah involved to some extent in all three. Furthermore, the Book is mainly composed of action, and the reader is much more consistently compelled by it, especially during the central crisis.

Hetty's story begins it, and we focus entirely on her for two chapters, as she becomes more and more desolate and destitute. We leave her at a stage where she is contemplating suicide and we know she is over seven months pregnant. The rest of her story is brought out cleverly in the course of the trial and what follows it. During the trial (Ch. 43) two witnesses tell first of the birth of the child, and then of Hetty's abandonment of it, and her discovery sitting forlorn where she had left it earlier. This gives the prosecution attitude, or what you might call the circumstantial evidence. Then after Dinah has calmed her, Hetty confesses and we hear her story (Ch. 45). The plot is therefore much more subtly developed than a straight account of a trial, in which both sides are put, could have been. Suspense is introduced by the gap between leaving Hetty in Chapter 37, Mr. Irwine's announcement of her arrest in Chapter 39, and the prosecution witnesses' accounts in Chapter 43; and we have two dramatic crises in place of one in Hetty's condemnation, and then her later confession. And yet this is only one strand of the construction at this stage.

Adam's story is equally dramatic. It begins with his fruitless search for Hetty in Snowfield and Stoniton (the names now take on a richer force) and his visit to Irwine who tells him of Hetty's arrest and crime. He is enraged and for long periods is not in control of his anger towards Arthur, but Irwine and subsequently Bartle Massey calm him and persuade him to a more measured attitude. The episode in Chapter 42 between him and Bartle Massey is one of the most important in the whole book. Adam is overcome by his helplessness in the face of 'irremediable evil and suffering'. This is a very necessary experience for Adam for 'It seemed to him as if he had always before thought it a light thing that men should suffer.' His was the kind of temperament that when confronted with suffering immediately attempted to rise out of it or to correct the wrong. In this instance, there is nothing he can do, and the suffering for him is intensified.

While he is in this state, Bartle Massey comes from the court, where, as yet, no judgment has been reached. Talking gently to Adam, and also allowing his simple compassion to be felt, Bartle brings Adam to agree to come into the court, and, which is rather important, to take some bread and wine. Whatever George Eliot's views may have been of the value of the sacrament, it is a species of sacrament she creates at this point, as an oblique confirmation of what has passed between Bartle and Adam. Bartle says of Mr. Irwine:

> 'Ah, it's a great thing in a man's life to be able to stand by a neighbour, and uphold him in such trouble as that.'
> 'God bless him, and you too, Mr. Massey,' said Adam, in a low voice, laying his hand on Bartle's arm.   Ch. 42

Not much is made of this episode; its symbolism, while obvious enough, is not as obtrusive as that of Dinah's arrival at the prison (see p. 69) and yet it is most important in the structure of the novel, and incidentally in relating this novel to the same running theme of the *Scenes of Clerical Life* (see pp. 73-7). Adam's story in this Book is completed after Hetty's reprieve when he and Arthur meet and are reconciled in Chapter 48.

Finally into this sequence is woven the third strand of Arthur. In Chapter 40 we hear, not unexpectedly, of Squire Donnithorne's death. Letters are sent to recall Arthur, and Irwine decides not to send a letter about Hetty to him, but leaves it for him to find when he gets home. This allows George Eliot the fine Chapter 44 in which we see Arthur's happy and hopeful return. He is even happy in his thoughts about Hetty since he has earlier heard that Adam and Hetty are engaged and he therefore reasonably supposes that the past is to some extent healed. Irwine's letter to Arthur is terse and the shock immediate. Arthur hastens to Stoniton and we do not hear of him again until he arrives with the reprieve. And in all this complex and flexible handling of dramatic and critical material, only that arrival fails. George Eliot resorts to the present historic and cannot avoid the false romanticism inherent in the whole episode. Nor is this impression obliterated when we later learn that Hetty is only saved from the gallows and is still to be deported. Nevertheless, when the sequence is considered: Hetty's flight and despair, Adam's search, Hetty's imprisonment, Squire Donnithorne's death, Adam's anger and later calm, Hetty's sentencing, Dinah's arrival at the prison, Hetty's moving confession, and the ride to the scaffold, it is very remarkable that George Eliot was able to maintain all that material so well and so effectively, both as a story, and as something with a more important meaning. From the point of Arthur's gallop to bring the reprieve at the last minute, the novel is less successful, and the whole of Book Six, which concerns Adam's realisation of his love for Dinah and his successful wooing of her, is written in a less compelling way. It seems to be a sort of reward to Adam for his enduring, and there is something uneasy in the incorporation of Dinah into the community, necessary though that is to the completion of the theme.

I have given this account of the construction of *Adam Bede*, partly because it is a remarkable achievement for a 'first' novel, and partly because it shows George Eliot's skills very well, and is easier to deal with than *The Mill on the Floss*, which is un-balanced, as the author herself admitted, or *Silas Marner*, which while well constructed is much simpler.

Characterisation

The really important characters in this novel for the reader who is concerned to get at George Eliot's most central interests are not the four main characters, but rather Mrs. Poyser (and to some extent her husband), Mr. Irwine, Lisbeth Bede and Bartle Massey. These are the characters of whom the truth is being told, and it is interesting that it is in connection with Mr. Irwine that George Eliot chooses to introduce her justification in Chapter 17 *In Which the Story Pauses a Little*. This is a chapter in which the author's persona speaks directly to the reader. To some extent, this persona is still the male one which recounted the *Scenes*, but regardless of that this statement is surely one to which George Eliot would thoroughly adhere:

> So I am content to tell my simple story, without trying to make things seem better than they were; dreading nothing, indeed, but falsity, which in spite of one's best efforts, there is reason to dread. Falsehood is so easy, truth so difficult. The pencil is conscious of a delightful facility in drawing a griffin—the longer the claws, and the larger the wings, the better; but that marvellous facility which we mistook for genius is apt to forsake us when we want to draw a real unexaggerated lion. Examine your words well, and you will find that even when you have no motive to be false, it is a very hard thing to say the exact truth, even about your own immediate feelings—much harder than to say something fine about them which is *not* the exact truth.   Ch. 17

This is the sort of author's comment for which George Eliot is notorious and which has been most frequently identified as one of her worst faults. Lately, however, there is a trend in criti-cal opinion which ceases to identify these intrusions as a fault. They can be, of course, but so equally can parts which are directly narrative or dramatic—success will depend on the place in the novel and how well they are written. I feel that the constant presence of George Eliot or indeed of Marian Evans in her novels almost always enhances them because of the sheer quality of her mind, even though there may be an interruption in the narrative. It is, of course, another characteristic that the 19th-century reader would have had time for. Professor Daiches gives a good assessment of the problem:

> The direct intervention of the author to enlarge the significance of an action may be disconcerting to some modern readers, but this kind of placing of a moment of the novel on the larger map of human morality and human feeling is perfectly appropriate and is reinforced by the novel's total movement [he is referring to a specific instance in *Middlemarch*]. George Eliot is not pressing on to an incident a meaning greater than it can bear; she is rather assisting the reader how to read properly by suggesting the wider context to which the novel refers. We may object that such assistance is unnecessary, and it is certainly true that on occasion it is so. But often it plays a part in sustaining the tone, in preventing any premature taking of sides, in clarifying the sorts of interest with which the story is presented to the reader, and in general in establishing a mutual commitment to moral and psychological exploration by both writer and reader.   MIDDLEMARCH, p. 38

In *Adam Bede*, she undoubtedly fulfills her pursuit of truth better in the characters I have mentioned than in her central characters, all of whom are in some way romanticised. In the other four, no pretence is made that there is anything specially admirable about them, indeed quite the opposite. Lisbeth Bede is a plaintive, worrying creature, who would undoubtedly get on anyone's nerves as she tends to get on Adam's, but her simple possessive love of her home and her sons and her understanding of them obliges sympathy, especially when this is indicated to us by Dinah's behaviour. Bartle Massey's misogyny is comic, as is his attitude to his bitch, Vixen, but his sympathy for Adam in his crisis is predictable, and the little exchange between him and Irwine is illuminating. Bartle has offered to go to Stoniton, and Irwine, whose image of Bartle is the one which the schoolmaster encourages by his words and behaviour, warns him:

'But . . . you must be careful what you say to him, you know. I'm afraid you have too little fellow-feeling in what you consider his weakness about Hetty.'

'Trust to me, sir—trust to me. I know what you mean. I've been a fool myself in my time, but that's between you and me. I shan't thrust myself on him—only keep my eye on him, and see that he gets some food, and put in a word here and there.' Ch. 40

I think we are meant to believe that there is somewhere in Bartle's past an experience of love which perhaps disappointed him but through which he has acquired his humanity, despite his irritable exterior. It would be totally characteristic of George Eliot to see all her characters in the round in this way.

Mrs. Poyser is a slightly more difficult character to judge because she is one of George Eliot's famous creations and is looked on with affection. She is indeed loquacious and somewhat comic with it. She is also overbearing and dominating in her home, and her outburst to the Squire is characteristic. She is possessive of Dinah. But the reality of her feeling for Dinah, and an indication of what weaknesses she has beneath the hard surface, are shown up in the episode of the broken jugs. She is forced by Molly's incompetence to get out the brown and white jug which she does not usually use. Just as she gets it out, Hetty appears at the doorway dressed as Dinah, because of something Adam has said to her. For a moment Mrs. Poyser thinks it is Dinah she sees, and in her shock drops the jug, thereby bringing on her own head the sort of remark she had just poured on the unfortunate Molly. She is not of course as self-reliant as she would seem, and her wish to keep Dinah near her is not just a case of parochial possessiveness. This too is the kind of episode which makes a character real.

Irwine is in fact analysed by George Eliot herself in the chapter quoted from (Ch. 17) and he is much more important than the other three. If this is a fourth *Scene* it centres to some extent on him. It is he who takes over during the crisis and has to bear the brunt of all the main characters' stresses, at least until Dinah arrives. He is very well done, because the reader is genuinely made to feel that he is not a satisfactory cleric, that he is somewhat lazy, somewhat unspiritual, and somewhat too interested in his worldly rather than his heavenly place. His strength at the end is an effective demonstration of what George Eliot has said of him in Chapter 17.

The four main characters can all be taken together, for they are all created with a falsifying romantic approach. Adam is a hero. He may have his faults analysed, his pride and his stiffness, and his short-sightedness both about Hetty and Dinah, but he is so strongly invested with heroic qualities of strength, upright-ness and good craftsmanship, that the glamour is never dispersed. Dinah is much the same; like Adam her appearance and de-meanour are constantly admired. They are both endowed with special power over others. They have what this century calls the charisma (the special power over others attributed for instance to the Kennedy family). Dinah's power is given more chances to reveal itself than Adam's especially in her calming effect both on Mrs. Poyser, and on Lisbeth Bede, but most particu-larly on Hetty in prison, and there is no doubt that this scene (Ch. 45) is one of the most compelling in the novel—especially for the reader who is not put off by the Evangelical terminology —and Hetty's confession is moving in any event.

Arthur and Hetty are both invested with a different kind of charisma. Where Adam and Dinah have moral grace, the other two have worldly grace. Arthur is young, gallant, well-meaning, honourable and charming. Hetty is pretty, and pretty in a very compelling way, and George Eliot dwells frequently on her beauty. Even when she pins the poor girl down as 'a little trivial soul' (Ch. 31), Hetty remains a helpless heroine figure lost in the sorrows of the world.

This problem of characterisation remained with George Eliot in almost every novel though it became less prominent. It is still strong in *The Mill on the Floss* where it falsifies especially Stephen Guest, but also to some extent Tom and Maggie Tulliver, and it is put to advantage in *Romola* where such a romantic viewpoint on character is much more appropriate. In the last three novels it is held more in control.

Conclusion

Adam Bede is unlike most other of George Eliot's novels, except *Silas Marner*, in that it does not have a sensitive and susceptible character near the centre, and it is so exclusively rural. Because of this it is in some ways the best controlled of all, despite the reservations about the main characters, and George Eliot does not again succeed in organising her material so completely in relation to her intentions until *Middlemarch*.

6

The Grand Experiments

Scenes of Clerical Life and *Adam Bede* were written largely out of George Eliot's memory, not so much of her personal experiences but of the whole context and way of life of her childhood. The *Scenes* are experiments on a comparatively small scale, while *Adam Bede* is a complete achievement and a controlled work of art within certain limits. These limits exclude both the higher modes of thought and feeling, the creation of characters whose defects are really unattractive, and the problems of poverty and of urban life. The novels of the period from 1859 to 1866 are all in their different ways experiments on a much grander scale. It is worth noting in passing that in her six major novels she never repeats an effect or a character or a major dramatic situation.

The three major novels of this period, *The Mill on the Floss*, *Romola* and *Felix Holt*, are all flawed, and their flaws are perhaps more prominent and damaging than any that adverse criticism can point out in *Adam Bede*. In this period she also published *Silas Marner*, which is generally held to be the best controlled of all her works, though it is much slighter, and two short stories, *Brother Jacob* and *The Lifted Veil*.

Brother Jacob, the story of David Faux, alias Edward Freely, who takes advantage of his idiot brother Jacob to steal his mother's money, but is later found out, just at the point when he hopes to make a profitable marriage, is a slight affair and would not now be read but for its author's reputation.

The Lifted Veil on the other hand is a strange story which a reader familiar with George Eliot would hardly expect, and which might almost be classed as science fiction. It is also the only one of her writings before *Daniel Deronda* which draws on her extensive experience of travel in Europe, another characteristic which differentiates it in tone from the rest of her work in this period. It is set in the middle years of the 19th century, and is told in the first person, the only occasion when George Eliot adopts this technique. The narrator is called Latimer and is endowed with extra-sensory perception. He has a vision of a scene in Prague long before he actually sees it, and he gradually becomes aware that he has extra-sensory powers, particularly towards his wife, in whom he sees hatred well before they are married, in fact while she is still engaged to his brother. The brother is killed and the woman marries Latimer. The end of the story is ghoulish. Latimer and his wife become estranged as predicted, although they continue to live together (an early echo here of Grandcourt and Gwendolen Harleth) and the wife hires a new maid. The maid becomes seriously ill with peritonitis and dies. Latimer has a doctor friend staying in the house who proposes to conduct a weird experiment on the dead woman's body immediately after her death, which is to transfuse into her his own blood. The transfusion revives the maid long enough for her to accuse the wife of intending to poison Latimer, an accusation she had been prevented from making before by the wife's continued presence at her bedside. It is a successful horror story and shows how well George Eliot could write in totally different modes. Both in style and atmosphere it has a more modern feeling than almost anything else she wrote, even though the idea of the reviving transfusion is not easy to accept. Latimer's extra-sensory perception is on the other hand very convincing still. Nor does the story lack some typical touches of George Eliot's sharper observation, especially in her comment on the barrenness of Latimer's marriage: 'The rich find it easy to live married and apart.'

'THE MILL ON THE FLOSS'

This has been perhaps George Eliot's best known novel until recent years, and largely because of the famous and extended portrayal of the childhood of Tom and Maggie Tulliver, most of which is recounted from their viewpoint, and also because Maggie Tulliver has been identified with Marian Evans. This identification is no more fruitful than looking for Jane Austen behind all of her most sympathetic heroines. It is not reasonable to suppose that a great writer creating a character who possesses some similar qualities to him- or her-self will be able thoroughly to disentangle that character from his own. One might just as well see Marian Evans in Dinah Morris or Dorothea Brooke, and yet a closer identification than any of these might be Mary Garth, whose father at least is much more obviously a portrait of Robert Evans. Maggie Tulliver is like George Eliot in her sensibility, but her family is quite different from the Evanses, unless the author was being utterly disrespectful to both her parents, which is impossible to suppose. Maggie's education is somewhat different, and unlike George Eliot she is quite incapable of making the necessary breach with her past which would have been her only means of salvation. Of course, she is *like* Marian Evans, but we do the writer no credit if we suppose that her vision of the character is blinkered by her preoccupation with a self-portrait.

The novel may also be regarded as one of the least well-made of the six major ones. It is heavily dominated by the personality of Maggie, and George Eliot is generally better when her attention is spread over several main characters. It is also heavily and at times rather obviously dominated by certain themes. Although George Eliot had determined to conclude it with the flood, and did a good deal of work to discover a town sited near a flooding river on which to base St. Oggs, she did not succeed in building the flood convincingly into the plot. It may be that there was no future for Maggie that was preferable to death, but her death under those circumstances remains an awkwardly contrived effect, especially when it is linked to her reunion with Tom. Their doom, which is closely related to the river, is hinted at earlier, but the river is not made into a great unifying symbol such as is to be found in Dickens's *Our Mutual Friend*. Finally the construction of the novel is looser and more episodic than *Adam Bede*, which also operates against a creative unity.

The story covers some eleven or twelve years of the period of George Eliot's own childhood, and takes Maggie from the age of about nine to her death at around twenty, and well over half of it is devoted to the detailed presentation of the Tullivers' childhood and their family life. Book Four is almost entirely analytical, and the last two have the effect of a separate narrative, describing Maggie's affair with Stephen. In some ways the best part of the novel is Book Five where the dividing fortunes of Tom and Maggie, and their inability to escape from the influences of the past on them, are brought out most effectively, especially in connection with Tulliver's assault on Wakem, and subsequent death.

The Flood

The river Floss and the flood are the dominating images of the novel, though it is not quite clear how far George Eliot meant them to be seen as such. Dorlcote Mill stands on the Floss as the Tullivers are placed in a particular and apparently unavoidable flow of life. They are doomed, as the river flows between certain banks, and are eventually overtaken by the stresses in their lives, as the river is by the flood. The particular character of their destiny is brought out in Book Five and discussed below.

Bessie Tulliver points up this theme early in the novel, following the episode in which Lucy Deane is pushed in the mud.

> 'They're such children for water, mine are,' she said aloud, without reflecting that there was no one to hear her; 'They'll be brought in dead and drownded some day. I wish that river was far enough.' Book I, Ch. 10

It is not made prominent again until much later when Philip dreams of Maggie falling down a waterfall (Book VI, Ch. 8), and then of course when the river carries Maggie and Stephen to the sea, with disastrous consequences for Maggie.

Apart from these specific references, of course, the rivers, Ripple and Floss, are always present in the story, and references are made to past floods, which in part prepare us for the finale.

The flood itself is well written, but the accident of Tom and Maggie being in a boat which is borne down by broken wooden machinery from the wharves is too convenient, and the final paragraph is very lame indeed. If one considers the capacity of many other incidents in the novels to move and grip a 20th-century audience, one finds it hard to believe that this passage would have moved any but the least discriminating of Victorian readers:

> The boat reappeared—but brother and sister had gone down in an embrace never to be parted: living through again in one supreme moment the days when they had clasped their little hands in love, and roamed the daisied fields together. Book VII, Ch. 5

Themes

There are four identifiable themes in this novel, all interrelated and all difficult to illustrate briefly. The two most prominent are the presentation of how far upbringing and background condition and in fact warp a growing personality, and of the quality of the particular background involved here, that is the society of the Dodsons and their like. These topics are part of the whole fabric of the novel. Less prominent but just as important are the two problems affecting Maggie—first that she is a woman, but does not behave as a woman of her time is expected to, and then her internal conflict, which takes on a much wider importance, between what she sees as duty and her own desires. The first of these themes accounts for the length of that part of the book which deals with Tom and Maggie's growing-up, and in fact George Eliot later regretted that she had had to increase the tempo in the later parts of the book. Her description of the children, of Maggie's temperament shown in incidents like the hair-cutting, and Tom's temper shown in his encounter with Bob over the pocket-knife, are very intimately related to the adult character of the two individuals, just as much as the more obvious early antipathy between Tom and Philip. It is, of course, no accident that Philip is physically deformed. His physical deformity has been overcome and the basic goodness of his character allowed to grow. Tom's goodness has been, one is tempted to say, systematically warped until at the end he is as mentally deformed as Philip is physically, despite his noble exterior.

It is the narrowness of this provincial life that is mainly responsible for this thwarting of Maggie, and warping of Tom, and this is a constant theme in the novel. From the very beginning when Mr. Tulliver decides to send Tom to a new school for which he is basically unsuited, the influence begins to work. Tulliver mistakenly considers a gentleman's education will be a good thing for his son. That it is not is savagely brought home when Tom goes to his uncle Deane and discovers that his accomplishments are quite unsuited to his needs.

However, George Eliot does not merely present this as a theme, and that is another purpose of the long description of the Tulliver and Dodson family life. We see the Dodsons in action and it is not until much later that their ethos is analysed.

This occurs at the beginning of Book Four, after the reader has had plenty of time to establish his own ideas about the limitations of Gleggs, Pullets, Deanes and Tullivers:

> It is a sordid life, you say, this of the Tullivers and Dodsons—
> irradiated by no sublime principles, no romantic visions, no active
> self-renouncing faith—moved by none of those wild uncontrollable
> passions which create the dark shadows of misery and crime—
> without that primitive rough simplicity of wants, that hard sub-
> missive, ill-paid toil, that child-like spelling out of what nature has
> written, which gives its poetry to peasant life. Here, one has
> conventional worldly notions and habits without instruction and
> without polish—surely the most prosaic form of human life:
> proud respectability in a gig of unfashionable build: worldliness
> without side-dishes. Observing these people narrowly, even
> when the iron hand of misfortune has shaken them from their
> unquestioning hold on the world, one sees little trace of religion,
> still less of a distinctly Christian creed. Their belief in the Unseen,
> so far as it manifests itself at all, seems to be rather of a pagan kind;
> their moral notions, though held with strong tenacity, seem to have
> no standard beyond hereditary custom. You could not live among
> such people; you are stifled for the want of an outlet towards some-
> thing beautiful, great, and noble; you are irritated with these dull

men and women, as a kind of population out of keeping with the earth on which they live—with this rich plain where the great river flows for ever onward, and links the small pulse of the old English town with the beatings of the world's mighty heart. A vigorous superstition, that lashes its gods or lashes its own back, seems to be more congruous with the mystery of the human lot, than the mental condition of these emmet-like Dodsons and Tullivers.

I share with you this sense of oppressive narrowness; but it is necessary that we should feel it, if we care to understand how it acted on the lives of Tom and Maggie—how it has acted on young natures in many generations.   IV, 1

This most explicitly defines George Eliot's purpose in at least the first half of the novel. She then goes on to define the qualities of the Dodsons in a passage which the reader is now able to relate to his experience of them not as a tribe but as widely differing individuals.

The religion of the Dodsons consisted in revering whatever was customary and respectable; it was necessary to be baptised, else one could not be buried in the churchyard, and to take the sacrament before death, as a security against more dimly understood perils; but it was of equal necessity to have the proper pall-bearers and well-cured hams at one's funeral, and to leave an unimpeachable will. A Dodson would not be taxed with the omission of anything that was becoming, or that belonged to that eternal fitness of things which was plainly indicated in the practice of the most substantial parishioners, and in the family traditions—such as obedience to parents, faithfulness to kindred, industry, rigid honesty, thrift, the thorough scouring of wooden and copper utensils, the hoarding of coins likely to disappear from the currency, the production of first-rate commodities for the market, and the general preference for whatever was home-made. The Dodsons were a very proud race, and their pride lay in the utter frustration of all desire to tax them with a breach of traditional duty of propriety. A wholesome pride in many respects, since it identified honour with perfect integrity, thoroughness of work, and faithfulness to admitted rules: and society owes some worthy qualities in many other members to mothers of the Dodson class, who made their butter and their fromenty well and would have felt disgrace to make it otherwise.

To be honest and poor was never a Dodson motto, still less to seem rich though being poor; rather, the family badge was to be honest and rich; and not only rich, but richer than was supposed. To live respected, and have the proper bearers at your funeral, was an achievement of the ends of existence that would be entirely nullified if on the reading of your will you sank in the opinion of your fellow-men, either by turning out to be poorer than they expected, or by leaving your money in a capricious manner, without strict regard to degrees of kin. The right thing must always be done towards kindred. The right thing was to correct them severely, if they were other than a credit to the family, but still not to alienate from them the smallest rightful share in the family shoe-buckles and other property. A conspicuous quality in the Dodson character was its genuineness: its vices and virtues alike were phases of proud, honest, egoism, which had a hearty dislike to whatever made against its own credit and interest, and would be frankly hard of speech to inconvenient kin, but would never forsake or ignore them—would not let them want bread, but only require them to eat it with bitter herbs.   IV, 1

All this we have been watching in action almost to the letter, both the strengths in Mr. Deane, and the weaknesses in Mrs. Pullet, and the mixture in Mrs. Glegg, who is the best example of the type, as is well shown in the episode between her and Bob Jakin over a question of muslin (Book V, Ch. 2), and then again when she offers support to Maggie in her distress at the end (Book VII, Ch. 3). And we are to see it now come to tragic fruit in Tom's honest and honourable boorishness, and Maggie's passionate self-destruction.

The Dodson male's attitude to women is of course that their place is in the home, and that they are not entitled to be educated above the level of millinery, and while this is a constant issue between Tom and Maggie because she will not in Tom's eyes behave as she ought ('Your ideas and mine will never accord, and you will never give way,' VI, 4), it is best shown up in Mr. Wakem's admittedly heated reaction to his son's love for Maggie (Book VI, Ch. 8). His first reaction in reference to Maggie is, 'We don't ask what a woman does, we ask who she belongs to.' However, he is in fact more than a Dodson, which points up the issue. When he is calmer later he comes to accept the possibility of Philip marrying Maggie, in total contrast to Tom's utter and unshakeable prejudice on that subject. When Lucy Deane tries to sway Tom on this, she meets the blankest of blank walls (Book VI, Ch. 12), and the author herself defines the nature of Tom's mind and its bent to inherited prejudice.

Maggie's sense of duty is also a product of her environment combined with certain chances along the way. She is well fitted by her life to find consolation in the self-denying faith of Thomas à Kempis (IV, 3). It comes out first in her tensions over meeting Philip in the Red Deeps. Here she declares her conviction of the necessity of duty to her parents and her family, and her whole response to Philip is made guilty by her sense that it must be secretive. To some extent the loss of the meetings is a relief just because the secrecy is ended:

> And yet, how was it that she was now and then conscious of a dim background of relief in the forced separation from Philip? Surely it was only because the sense of a deliverance from conceal-ment was welcome at any cost.   V, 5

Then the issue reappears much more strongly over Stephen Guest. Here, Maggie is torn first of all by her sense of loving him in a different way from loving Philip, and in a more demanding way. In this case the conflict of duty is obvious because she owes it directly to Lucy not to allow her affair with Stephen to develop. At first she is able to carry out her purpose as she describes it to Stephen outside Aunt Moss's:

> 'Oh, it is difficult—life is very difficult! It seems right to me sometimes that we should follow our strongest feelings; but then, such feelings continually come across the ties that all our former life had made for us—the ties that have made others dependent on us—and would cut them in two. If life were quite easy and simple as it might have been in Paradise, and we could always see that one being first towards whom . . . I mean if life did not make duties for us before love comes, love would be a sign that two people ought to belong to each other. But I see—I feel it is not so now: there are things we must renounce in life; some of us must resign

love. Many things are difficult and dark to me; but I see one thing quite clearly—that I must not, cannot, seek my own happiness by sacrificing others. Love is natural; but surely pity and faithfulness and memory are natural too. And they would live in me still, and punish me if I did not obey them. I should be haunted by the suffering I had caused. Our love would be poisoned.'   VI, 11

However, her weakness, and fatal circumstances, conspire to create a much greater crisis after she has spent the enforced night with Stephen away from St. Oggs and is faced with the choice of going on with him, or returning to calumny and suffering. The plotting of this whole sequence is not one of George Eliot's best achievements. The characterisation of Stephen is weak, partly because we have not been allowed to see his character develop, and it is not as we see it very convincing. His jugglings with conscience are less acceptable even than Arthur Donnithorne's. Furthermore the accidents whereby Stephen and Maggie are alone in the boat and obliged to spend a night together are too contrived. However, the crisis of choice is very real. Stephen attempts to convince her that they are being driven by stronger forces than the ties of duty. He says 'natural law surmounts every other; we can't help what it clashes with'. And Maggie's reply is the completion of her earlier statement now broadened to an almost philosophical plane:

'It is not so, Stephen—I'm quite sure that is wrong. I have tried to think it again and again; but I see, if we judged in that way, there would be a warrant for all treachery and cruelty—we should justify breaking the most sacred ties that can ever be formed on earth. If the past is not to bind us, where can duty lie? We should have no law but the inclination of the moment.'   VI, 14

And so she goes back to face the scorn of her friends, her family, and the town. She is befriended by Dr. Kenn who tries at first to repel the cruel prejudices against her until these start to fall on him, so that he too has to desert her. The analysis of the town's reaction (VII, 2) with regard to what would have been said if she had gone off with Stephen—ironically and tragically a gradual acceptance, provided they had married—and (VII, 5) the analysis of the town's reaction to Dr. Kenn taking on Maggie as governess are further examples of George Eliot's purpose of concentrating at every point on the cruel stultification of the provincial mentality.

Construction

The basic construction of *The Mill on the Floss* is merely chronological, spread over some eleven years. The gradual presentation of the Tullivers' childhood is interrupted abruptly after Mr. Tulliver's collapse, and Book Four is largely an analysis of what has gone before and an account of Maggie's state of mind under the pressure of suffering. Book Five seems to be the only one that has been substantially organised to create a particular effect at the end, that is not fully identified by the author herself, although her purpose is indicated by the title of the Book, *Wheat and Tares*, and by the aphorism in Chapter 7, 'Mingled seed must bear a mingled crop'. The Book begins with Maggie's meeting Philip in the Red Deeps and their discussion of her responsibility to herself and to her family. This is balanced in the next chapter by Tom's first step forward out of the collapse of his father. He goes with Bob to the Gleggs to get capital for his venture in trading. The next two chapters develop Maggie's love for Philip over a year, based only on their meetings in the Red Deeps and therefore for her if not for Philip an unreal experience in the deeper levels of her life. Chapter Five brings the exposure, by accident only. Aunt Pullet has seen Philip come out of the Red Deeps and says so in Tom's hearing, who, suspicious as he is, sees the connection. He challenges Maggie, and goes with her to the woods where he coarsely and brutishly insults Philip. This is the point at which he appears most objectionable, and the reader is gratified by Maggie's rebuke of him subsequently. Her joy then is mixed quickly with sorrow. Directly after this, Tom shows that he has made enough money to pay off Tulliver's debts, which he does. The family are overjoyed, and Tom 'never lived to taste another moment so delicious' (Ch. 6). Maggie too is happy and respects Tom for what he has done. But Tulliver has not changed, and when the chance arises he thrashes Wakem, which brings on an attack and he shortly dies. So Tom's joy is quickly mixed with sorrow. As well as the remark about mingled seed, George Eliot is even more explicit:

> Apparently the mingled thread in the web of their life was so curiously twisted together, that there could be no joy without a sorrow coming close upon it. V, 7

That is the fate of the Tullivers which the river symbolises.

Among Tulliver's dying words he says 'I was good to *my* sister' while he is giving Maggie into Tom's charge. And he was indeed, for even in extremity he would not call in the £300 which the Mosses owed him. This was a good thread among the many weak or bad. But ironically it is not a good thread handed on to Tom, who not only is not good to his sister, but makes very little attempt to understand her.

The rest of the novel is devoted to the much more explicit narrative of Maggie's affair with Stephen Guest and its tragic outcome.

Characterisation

A good deal has already been said in passing about the characterisation in this novel. Some of it is a direct continuation of the type of characterisation seen in *Adam Bede*, though there are fewer minor characters to enrich the scene. Maggie and Philip both represent a development into characters of rich and complex sensibility, and Philip is one of her more memorable studies of a character born to weakness in one way, and yet endowed with particular strengths which help him to live with his weaknesses. However, Bessie and Edward Tulliver are really more important, because they are not only weak, they are positively wrongheaded. Bessie makes two mistakes which both have dreadful consequences for her family. First it is she who urges her husband to write to Mrs. Glegg to say that he will repay the £500 he owes her, at a time when we know she is not going to call it in, and when a man of better judgment would have waited a bit. Secondly, it is she who puts into Wakem's head the idea that he might buy the Mill, thus completing Tulliver's sense of shame, and creating the resentment which subsequently brings about her husband's death. He is equally wrong-headed, in his expectations for Tom, in his financial affairs, and in his legal affairs, and once the catastrophe has occurred he is a broken man, possessed only of one idea, to get his own back on Wakem. With these two characters there is a feeling that if George Eliot were to withdraw her sympathy from anyone it would be from such as these. She shows them as foolish and obstinate, and she shows the consequences of their folly both for themselves and for their children. In no other novel does she put this type of folly at the centre of the work, nor with such tragic consequences. This is her first attempt at a fully tragic novel, and although the tragic conclusion of the narrative is not a success, the tragedy of Tom and Maggie Tulliver is all too clear, flood or no flood.

'SILAS MARNER'

Silas Marner is a much simpler work than any other of George Eliot's. It is more of a fable than a novel, in which the central topic is the replacement of Marner's dead gold with the living gold of his adopted daughter, Eppie. The purpose of the novel is to show the regeneration of Marner's personality by the influence of the child. As he looks after her, and as she grows up, Marner becomes a fuller and warmer human being than the one who had been destroyed, first by the lies which had driven him from Lantern Yard, and then by the theft of his gold, which had been the single love of his life for fifteen years of weaving in Raveloe.

The story has much more in common with *Scenes of Clerical Life* and *Adam Bede* than with the the later novels, firstly because its theme is the regeneration of the spirit and of mere human confidence by the sympathetic contact with others, in this case Eppie, but also Dollie and Aaron Winthrop; and secondly because Raveloe is a community that has more in common with Hayslope and Broxton than with St. Oggs. The minor characters and the scene in the inn when Silas announces the theft of his gold are more like scenes in the early novels; and the New

Year's party at Squire Cass's resembles Arthur Donnithorne's birthday party.

At the same time, it has at least three important characteristics which reveal something both of the author's development and of the themes she is turning towards. It is written more concisely both in style and form. It has a well controlled plot of which none of the important events is at all improbable, given the community and the characters, which are sketched in more economically than usual. In particular, we are told enough of Dunsey Cass to believe entirely in his behaviour following the sale of the horse Wildfire, both with regard to the accident in which Wildfire is killed, and to the theft of the gold and subsequent fall into the Stone Pit. Similarly of Godfrey Cass, if we are not quite convinced of the reasons which led him to marry Molly Farren, his behaviour towards Nancy, and then over Eppie is convincing. However, the characters are not as whole or rich as those of the major novels, and it is clear that George Eliot has deliberately reduced the story to the shape of a fable, in which Silas gets what he deserves because he took in Eppie on the critical, and symbolic, New Year's Eve, while Godfrey gets what he deserves because he did not.

Silas himself is a good example of the author's capacity to make fully sympathetic a character, like Amos Barton, who has very little to recommend himself. Of the other characters, Eppie and Godfrey are the most interesting because they are the first instances of two subjects which engross George Eliot in *Romola* and in *Felix Holt*. In *Silas Marner* and the other two novels one central character is faced with the problem of responsibility towards a foster-parent, Eppie to Silas, Esther Lyon to Rufus, and Tito Melema to Baldassarre, and the problem is also examined when Harold Transome is faced with the fact that Matthew Jermyn is his father. In Eppie's case, the solution is a simple one, because she is set in a fable. She quickly chooses the father who took her in rather than the one who rejected her for his own selfish motives when he had the chance to acknowledge her.

Godfrey Cass is a forerunner of Tito in his capacity for

dissimulation. He is not a bad man, but his weaknesses have led him to lies from which he cannot now escape, and this statement which follows Godfrey's remarks about missing the dancing to come out and see Mollie is highly relevant to the much fuller portrait of Tito Melema:

> The prevarication and white lies which a mind that keeps itself ambitiously pure is as uneasy under as a great artist under the false touches that no eye detects but his own, are worn as lightly as mere trimmings when once the actions have become a lie. Ch. 13

A final point about *Silas Marner* is that the author is much defter in her interpretative remarks. The self-conscious narrator is not present here, and comments are limited to such as just quoted, or put into the mouths of the characters such as Dolly Winthrop:

> '. . . and everything else is a big puzzle to me when I think on it. For there was the fever come and took off them as were full-growed, and left the helpless children; and there's the breaking o' limbs; and them as 'ud do right and be sober have to suffer by them as are contrairy—eh, there's trouble i' this world, and there's things as we can niver make out the rights on.' Ch. 16

The speech from which this is taken is much longer than this and is to be sure a sermon of sorts, and not quite what one might expect from such a person as Dolly Winthrop, at least as far as its organisation is concerned. But it is thoroughly in keeping with the whole concept of the novel, and what she says is borne out by what happens.

'ROMOLA'

Romola presents the biggest problem for a critic of George Eliot. To dismiss it as a heroic failure is not enough, but an adequate approach to it requires not only the effort of studying it in depth, but also the acquisition of a large amount of 15th-century Italian history, and general knowledge of the Renaissance. It also needs to be set in the context of the historical novel of the 19th century, a very popular form indeed. Such an examination of this novel is beyond the scope of the present study.

However, there are a few important features of *Romola* which are relevant to a general understanding of George Eliot's writing.

The Scale of 'Romola'

Romola is written on a much grander scale than anything George Eliot had written before it, and without it she might have lacked the skill and experience to cope with the scale of her last three novels. It is a novel in which broad political themes are interwoven with the fortunes of individuals, much in the same way, though much less successfully, as Conrad relates these things in *Nostromo*. The complex Florentine political scene is not just a backcloth to the private story, it is an important formal part of the novel, as is the conflict of attitude between the humanist scholar Bardo di Bardi, Romola's father, who regards the church as a hotbed of superstition and fantasy, and that same church as it is represented to him in his son Dino, who is a monk, and the Dominican monk, Savonarola. Romola's life is the working out of this conflict. At first she is devoted to her father, and rejects Dino's sinister forebodings of what will become of her as superstitious. Later, under the oppressive influence of Savonarola, she is converted to Christianity. Finally, when she sees the monk's limitations, she breaks from him and stands for her own values at last. Savonarola, in words common to all leaders who believe in their cause, says to her, 'The cause of my party is the cause of God's kingdom,' to which she replies, 'I do not believe it. God's kingdom is something wider—else let me stand outside it with the beings that I love' (Ch. 59). She departs from Florence in a disillusioned state:

> The vision of any great purpose, any end of existence which could ennoble endurance and exalt the common deeds of a dusty life with divine ardours, was utterly eclipsed for her now by the sense of a confusion in human things which made all effort a mere dragging of tangled threads; all fellowship either for resistance or advocacy, mere unfairness and exclusiveness.

She is brought out of this state of mind by her chance arrival in a village beset by plague, where she is able to help restore

hope and health—she has for some years been working among the
sick in Florence. Later, she returns to Florence and finds some
peace of mind in caring for her husband's other 'wife' and his
two children. This conflict in Romola between the great influences on her life, her father, her husband and Savonarola,
indicates, if rather heavily, how important to George Eliot is the
search for values. Dinah Morris had a firm set of values which
were clearly not enough to provide a complete answer for her
creator's speculative mind. Maggie Tulliver is tragically torn
between two sets of values, but is bound up with the lesser set—
the Dodson values—without being able to conform to them.
Romola's search is closer to George Eliot's own, and is cast in
a wider field of ideas, in the conflict between human and spiritual
values, and she reaches an answer that will do—help to alleviate
suffering wherever you can, and preserve an unswerving
devotion to the people you love and to those who need and
depend on you. Dorothea Brooke and Daniel Deronda continue
the search.

The other aspect of the scale of *Romola* which is important
is the magnitude of some of its scenes. George Eliot has shown
a liking for grand scenes several times before—the mockery of
Tryan, Arthur Donnithorne's birthday party, and the New Year
party at Squire Cass's have been the most successful. *Romola*
is full of such scenes, and they are rewarding for the patient
reader who is prepared simply to watch and listen without
worrying about the story too much. There is the Festival of
St. John the Baptist (Ch. 8), the Peasants' Fair on the Nativity
of the Virgin (Ch. 14), the Carnival (Ch. 20), the entry of
Charles VIII of France into Florence, a day which is allowed to
fill seven chapters (21–27); on a smaller scale but presented in
similar expansive detail, the dinner party at which Baldassarre
confronts Tito and is denied (Ch. 39), the procession of the
Madonna of the Impruneta into Florence to intercede for relief
from famine (Ch. 43), the execution of the five supporters of
the Medici (Ch. 60), the abortive Ordeal by Fire (Ch. 65),
the hunting of Tito (Ch. 67), and the execution of Savonarola
(Ch. 71). These are all memorable scenes involving large numbers

of people, something that is absent from Jane Austen and the Brontës and not common in Dickens, and they form the staple of this novel, though it is also enlivened with smaller occasions, of which the most memorable are the joke played on the quack doctor Tacco (Ch. 16) and the stripping of Monna Brigida at the hands of Savonarola's Red Army (Ch. 51). There are characters too who live in the fabric of the novel in an entirely natural way, playing their part in the working out of the story, when its main events happen to come their way, but never seeming to be devices because the scale of the novel is large enough to take them in as part of the Florentine scene. Of these, the most memorable and important are the barber Nello, whose shop is a centre for the exchange of news and views, the pedlar Bratti, who because he is itinerant sees and knows most of what goes on in Florence in high places and low, and the painter Piero di Cosimo, who sees more in things and people than most do, and whose paintings reveal truth before it is known, but who is also taciturn and kind.

Tito Melema

Of all the main characters, Tito is the most important. It is not common for novelists to undertake the portrayal of the systemmatic moral decay of a person who is basically kind and charming and good, until he becomes entirely selfish and corrupt. Again, this is something which required the wide scope of the novel and its large time scale if it was to succeed.

We follow Tito's history from 9 April 1492, when he arrives almost destitute in Florence, until 8 April 1498, when, as Secretary to the Ten, he is hunted down by the Compagnacci of Dolfo Spini, escapes by diving into the Arno, and is strangled by his foster-father Baldassarre. Broadly speaking, his whole history is a romance, and we are not under any obligation in this novel, as we are in the English ones, to judge by the most stringent standards of realism. This applies also to our judgment of Romola herself, and of Savonarola.

When he first arrives, he impresses everyone, except Piero di Cosimo, and later Bernardo del Nero, with his great physical beauty and his charm. He is fluent of speech, confident, adaptable and easy-going. He impresses himself in very different ways in the two spheres in which his life is lived. He convinces Bardo of his scholarship, and behaves in a perfectly judged way towards him, and to Romola, to whom he eventually manages to declare his love in a moment when they have both gone to fetch a book for the old scholar (Ch. 12). At the same time he becomes accidentally involved with the peasant-girl Tessa, whom he saves from a rough incident in the market, and then goes through a mock marriage which she believes in, and which he cannot bring himself to expose to her. Tessa's naïvety is convincing enough for this failure of Tito's to be credible. All through this part of the novel (Chs. 1–20) Tito is broadly attractive to the reader too, which is an important effect for it forces one to continue to view him sympathetically later. There are, however, hints of his weaknesses. Bernardo del Nero says of him in Chapter 7:

> 'That pretty Greek has a lithe sleekness about him, that seems marvellously fitted for slipping easily into any nest he fixes his mind on.'

A little later, after Nello has seen him signal to Tessa in the crowd, about which he has been evasive, the author says:

> Tito had an innate love of reticence—let us say a talent for it— which acted as other impulses do, without any conscious motive, and, like all people to whom concealment is easy, he would now and then conceal something which had as little the nature of a secret as the fact that he had seen a flight of crows.   Ch. 9

What gradually emerges of Tito is his lack of any standard except that of self-gratification, the pursuit of pleasure, and the avoidance of unpleasantness. This is what leads him to neglect his duty to his foster-father, to sell the ring, and eventually to deny Baldassarre to his face, when the old man turns up in Florence after Tito has lived there successfully for two years, and been married to Romola for one. After this time Tito gradually deteriorates, becoming estranged from Romola,

especially over the sale of her father's library, which he had
wished made over to the state, and becoming increasingly
involved in political intrigue, in which he operates as a treble
agent keeping contact in all three political arenas, the popular
party, the Medici party, and Savonarola's party. However,
George Eliot keeps alive the consciousness in Tito of what might
have happened and thus keeps before us the genuine ambiguity
of his character. After he rejects Baldassarre at the dinner, she
comments:

> 'Nay, so distinct sometimes is the working of a double conscious-
> ness within us, that Tito himself, while he triumphed in the appa-
> rent verification of his lie, wished that he had never made it necessary
> to himself—wished he had recognised his father on the steps—
> wished he had gone to seek him—wished everything had been
> different.'   Ch. 49

It is appropriate to comment at this point on George Eliot's
method of presenting such equivocal states of mind as this.
Objections are frequently made to her method of immediate
analysis of her characters' state of mind. It is however difficult to
see how any author would easily express the mingled condition
of mind, and the gradual changing of minds that George Eliot
attempts to portray without having recourse to at least some
measure of analytical comment, and it is one of her special contributions to the form of the novel that her characters were
presented in this degree of depth and breadth. She does not always
do it felicitously; for example, following the passage quoted
above about Tito comes a much less well-handled idea:

> But he had borrowed from the terrible usurer Falsehood, and the
> loan had mounted and mounted with the years, till he belonged to
> the usurer, body and soul.

The personification is awkward, and the tone inflated.

Tito's whole career in Florence is finally summed up by
Romola herself in talking to his son Lillo in the Epilogue:

> 'There was a man to whom I was very near, so that I could see
> a great deal of his life, who made almost everyone fond of him,
> for he was young, and clever, and beautiful, and his manners to

all were gentle and kind. I believe when I first knew him, he never thought of anything cruel or base. But because he tried to slip away from everything that was unpleasant, and cared for nothing else so much as his own safety, he came at last to commit some of the basest deeds—such as make men infamous. He denied his father, and left him to misery; he betrayed every trust that was reposed in him, that he might keep himself safe and get rich and prosperous. Yet calamity overtook him.'

In Tito Melema, George Eliot develops some ideas tried out in Godfrey Cass, and also gives another version of the behaviour of an individual towards a foster-father. Romola constantly sees this as the worst of Tito's crimes, that he forsook Baldassarre. It gradually becomes clear that the reality of acquired ties of love and duty is a most important element of George Eliot's thinking. In both *Silas Marner* and *Romola* the treatments of this problem are simple: Eppie does right and Tito wrong. In *Felix Holt* the theme is elaborated much more fully, and the pull on Esther Lyon is much more difficult to explain simply.

The best part of *Romola* is the section just before Romola leaves Florence for the second time (Chs. 57–61). In these chapters there is a full analysis of Tito's Machiavellian behaviour, followed by a final confrontation with Romola in which she tells him that she wishes to leave him. She then goes to Savonarola to plead with him to intercede on behalf of Bernardo del Nero, which he refuses to do. This interview shakes her free of the monk's power, and after watching Bernardo's execution, she leaves Florence. These five chapters bring to a crisis the various strands of her life, and are successful chiefly because we know so much of what has gone towards them.

In reading *Romola*, one can feel the continuous weight of the intellectual effort and control which it required. The patterns in the story work themselves out too geometrically, and one can understand the author's relief when she killed Tito in 1863 'in great excitement' and no doubt found herself in sight of the end. The scene in question is one of the greater failures in the novel because we have been anticipating it for so long, and it could hardly be other than the melodrama it is.

Often regarded as the weakest of George Eliot's novels, *Felix Holt* does not suffer from the limited viewpoint of *Adam Bede*, nor the constructional and other failures of *The Mill on the Floss*. It benefits greatly from the more complex character relationships that George Eliot has begun to develop, and also from her experience of writing the great panoramic scenes of *Romola*. It has a new type of character magnificently portrayed—Mrs. Transome—and is an experiment in the mystery story type of plot favoured by Dickens, in which the reader is given a constant series of clues and hints towards the eventual unravelling of a complication of relationships and inheritances. It is flawed chiefly in the character of Felix Holt himself who remains a blueprint rather than flesh and blood.

The Mystery of the Transome Inheritance

The development of this element of the story is what preoccupies much of George Eliot's attention in this novel, and what for some readers diminishes the novel's quality, although it must also be said that the elementary appeal of the mystery gives it an attraction which the broader stories of some of the other novels do not have. It was also experience towards the presentation of the story of Bulstrode, which is one of the major parts of *Middlemarch*.

The two elements of the mystery are presented differently. The secret in the past of Mrs. Transome over the paternity of her son Harold is not kept from the reader. There are numerous hints from very early in the book that his father is the lawyer Matthew Jermyn. The hidden background of Esther Lyon and her claim to the Transome estates is on the other hand kept from the reader. It soon emerges that she is not Rufus Lyon's real daughter, but her other connections are allowed to emerge slowly, and for example, when Mr. Christian, alias Henry Scaddon, goes to Mr. Lyon to claim his lost property, the reader as well as Mr. Lyon is allowed to suppose that *he* might be Esther's father.

The problem of the inheritance is not as complicated as the

legal terminology of it suggests, and a small plan helps to clarify it:

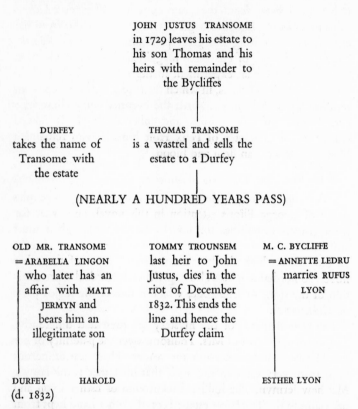

DURFEY FAMILY	TRANSOME FAMILY	BYCLIFFE FAMILY
	JOHN JUSTUS TRANSOME in 1729 leaves his estate to his son Thomas and his heirs with remainder to the Bycliffes	
DURFEY takes the name of Transome with the estate	THOMAS TRANSOME is a wastrel and sells the estate to a Durfey	

(NEARLY A HUNDRED YEARS PASS)

| OLD MR. TRANSOME = ARABELLA LINGON who later has an affair with MATT JERMYN and bears him an illegitimate son | TOMMY TROUNSEM last heir to John Justus, dies in the riot of December 1832. This ends the line and hence the Durfey claim | M. C. BYCLIFFE = ANNETTE LEDRU marries RUFUS LYON |
| DURFEY (d. 1832)   HAROLD | | ESTHER LYON |

Note: This plan is not intended to clarify the inheritance for those who have not read the novel, but may be helpful to those who are mystified while reading it.

So long as there is a living heir to Thomas Transome, the Durfeys' claim to the estate holds, but after that time, in other words when old Tommy Trounsem is trampled to death in the election riot at Treby, any living heir to the Bycliffes has a prior claim on the estate. This is hard for Harold Transome who has waited for the death of his wastrel elder brother to allow his claim to the estate. It is even harder when he discovers that he has no proper claim by birth since he is not old Mr. Transome's son.

The remaining complication concerns Mr. Christian, whose real name is Henry Scaddon. He squandered an inheritance in his youth, and went abroad in the army to escape disgrace. While a prisoner of the French, he changed places with Bycliffe in order that the latter could escape back to his wife Annette.

When Bycliffe, disguised as Scaddon, returns to England, he becomes the prey of Matthew Jermyn, who, protecting the Transome estates for Mrs. Transome from the Bycliffe claim, has him put in prison for the crimes of the real Scaddon, where he dies. Scaddon, calling himself Maurice Christian, eventually returns to England as servant to Philip Debarry, and finds himself possessed of useful information which he uses to make himself a thousand pounds from Harold Transome.

George Eliot was obviously intrigued by the manipulation of this plot, which shows a debt to *Bleak House* and to Dickens in general, and apart from the coincidental arrival in 1832 in the district of Treby of the four most important parties, Esther, Harold, Scaddon and Tommy Trounsem, she handles it skilfully, and uses it in a more meaningful way than Dickens does. For example, when the mystery is very nearly made clear to everybody, Jermyn's control of its unravelling, which he has wished to use at a particular time, is undermined on one side by Scaddon who tells Harold, and on the other side by Mr. Johnson who informs Esther. Both these events are consequences of Jermyn's treatment of the other two men, and deftly bring on the nemesis which pursues the lawyer, and Mrs. Transome. Harold gains confidence from the knowledge and the opportunity of marrying Esther, which he is sure he can achieve, and becomes once more fearless in his intention to expose Jermyn. He refuses to see the lawyer, who is forced to intrude upon a public meeting where he is driven finally to tell Harold that he is his father.

Mrs. Transome

Mrs. Transome is the most memorable character in *Felix Holt*, and the only full-scale portrait of a woman of her age and type that George Eliot attempts. Also here there seems to be some influence of Dickens, who had created in the last ten years such memorable elderly women as Lady Dedlock, Mrs. Clennam and Miss Havisham. Mrs. Transome escapes the melodrama, sometimes of action, and always of atmosphere, which makes those figures less successful. While her temperament has fitted her to be a woman active in the affairs of her family, she has been thwarted in this because of her weak husband and profligate elder son. She is full of hope when Harold returns, and the disappointment she suffers when she finds he does not see her in any other light than elegantly decorative and not to be involved in practical matters is very intense. In portraying this George Eliot relies much more than she has before on slight incidents during their early encounters—her reactions for example to Harold's remarks about the place of women: 'They interfere with a man's life. I shall not marry again' (a statement which circumstances force him to go back on).

> Mrs. Transome bit her lip and turned away to draw up the blind. She would not reply to words which showed how completely any conception of herself and her feelings was excluded from her son's inward world. Ch. 1

Or later, when she is driven rather further by his remark on women 'It doesn't signify what they think—they are not called upon to judge or to act.' To this she replies:

> 'I don't know who would be a mother if she could foresee what a slight thing she will be to her son when she is old.' Ch. 2

This bitterness remains all through the novel, and its most successful moments are when Mrs. Transome is forced by circumstances to swallow her pride, such as when she takes Jermyn's arm in Chapter 9, or when she goes with Harold to visit Esther in Malthouse Yard, after they know that their possession of the estate is in jeopardy (Ch. 38). The final chapters of the book, like the opening ones, are strengthened by the concentration on her. Her shocked disappointment begins the novel, and the final fatal blow when her son discovers the truth about Jermyn ends it, although George Eliot gives her the slight relief of Esther's compassion. This is not sentimental but serves to intensify the pathos of Mrs. Transome's life by bringing out the fearful absence of human affection in it. Her most terrible moment is her savage indictment of Jermyn, when he comes to persuade her to tell Harold about him. This is the only occasion when George Eliot portrays a woman of commanding temperament and great pride in a state of anger.

'Don't speak!' Mrs. Transome said peremptorily. 'Don't open your lips again. You have said enough; I will speak now. I have made sacrifices too, but it was when I knew that they were not my happiness. It was after I saw that I *had* stopped—after I saw that your tenderness had turned into calculation—after I saw that you cared for yourself only, and not for me. I heard your explanations—of your duty in life—of our mutual reputation—of a virtuous young lady attached to you. I bore it; I let everything go; I shut my eyes; I might almost have let myself starve, rather than have scenes of quarrel with the man I had loved, in which I must accuse him of turning my love into a good bargain.' There was a slight tremor in Mrs. Transome's voice in the last words, and for a moment she paused; but when she spoke again, it seemed as if the tremor had frozen into a cutting icicle. 'I suppose if a lover picked one's pocket, there's no woman would like to own it. I don't say I was not afraid of you. I *was* afraid of you, and I know now I was right.'

'Mrs. Transome,' said Jermyn, white to the lips, 'it is needless to say more. I withdraw any words that have offended you.'

'You can't withdraw them. Can a man apologise for being a dastard? . . . And I have caused you to strain your conscience, have I?—it is I who have sullied your purity? I should think the demons have more honour—they are not so impudent to one another. I would not lose the misery of being a woman, now I see what can be the baseness of a man. One must be a man—first to tell a woman that her love has made her your debtor, and then ask her to pay you by breaking the last poor threads between her and her son.'   Ch. 42

This is the voice of a discriminating and sensitive moral nature forced at last against itself to expose the crude moral vulgarity of what is opposed to it. While that vulgarity will never shrink from assaulting the sensitive, since it cannot know what sensibility is, the sensibility will seldom except under extreme pressure, such as here, descend to bandy words with the vulgar nature which can never really understand it. This encounter tells more of what George Eliot really admires in human nature than almost any other.

Of the other characters, Harold Transome and Jermyn are the most interesting, since each one takes up a facet of Tito Melema. Jermyn's personality is illustrated by an anecdote which fits Tito equally well:

A German poet was intrusted with a particularly fine sausage, which he was to convey to the donor's friend in Paris. In the course of a long journey he smelt the sausage; he got hungry, and desired to taste it; he pared a morsel off, then another, and another, in successive moments of temptation, till at last the sausage was, humanly speaking, at an end. The offence had not been premeditated. The poet had never loved meanness, but he loved sausage; and the result was undeniably awkward.   Ch. 9

Harold picks up the other side of Tito's nature, his love of pleasure, but he is much less objectionable, because, although he is a 'clever, frank, good-natured egoist', neither his character nor his circumstances lead him into anything more morally reprehensible than his failure to understand his mother.

There is in connection with Harold Transome's view of women an interesting cross-reference to Felix Holt's view, which is quite different. This type of casual cross-reference increases in scope in the later novels and is particularly prominent in *Daniel Deronda*. Felix, like Harold, does not intend to marry because he believes that women drag men down by their pettiness. He says, 'That's what makes women a curse; all life is stunted to suit their littleness' (Ch. 10). It is clear that his experience of women has not included such a one as Mrs. Transome. Harold wants women to be trivial and frivolous and has a mother who is far from that. Felix regrets that women are so trivial and frivolous and encounters one that as far as he can see is just that. The ironical connection is no simple opposite.

The Political Background

Felix Holt himself is best examined in connection with the political subject of the novel, the Reform Act riots of 1832. The novel deals with the period from 1 September 1832 until the Loamford assizes in the following spring, and the author has the same assurance in handling the important times that she showed in *Adam Bede*. Chapters 1–9 deal chiefly with three days in September and the consequences of Harold's homecoming. Chapters 10–22 cover five days in October and the development of the electioneering and the unravelling of the mystery. (Incidentally, George Eliot appears to make an unusual though wholly unimportant mistake in her time scheme. The 2 October 1832 was a Tuesday, not a Sunday.) The rest of the book covers a few days in November, the days in December of the Nominations, and of the Election itself, and the period just before and after Felix's trial for manslaughter. Her political interest is best defined in Chapter 3.

> These social changes in Treby parish are comparatively public matters, and this history is chiefly concerned with the private lot of a few men and women; but there is no private life which has not been determined by a wider public life . . .'

This and the fact that all lives are a consequence of their past are the dominant background ideas in this novel as in most of her others. *Felix Holt* is the first to have an epigraph for every chapter. These are sometimes illuminating, and sometimes not, though always relevant. When they are not attributed it can be assumed that they are the author's own. Two are particularly appropriate to our immediate context. Chapter 21 has:

'Tis grievous, that with all the amplifications of travel both by sea and land, a man can never separate himself from his past history.

Chapter 48 has:

'Tis law as steadfast as the throne of Zeus—
Our days are heritors of days gone by.   Aeschylus: AGAMEMNON

With regard to the immediate political problems, George Eliot is much more interested in the human connotations than the merely political attitudes. The novel is more about how and why electioneering is corrupt, and how and why the riots came about, and how Felix became involved in such a tragic way. There is only one episode when political ideas are foremost, which is when Felix goes to the nominations and is drawn into a speech. He makes it in response to a professional speech calling for what the Working Men's Association demanded in the People's Charter of 1838. The precise phrasing of his final sentence gives it an anachronistic ring, but undoubtedly these things were called for before the Charter was drawn up:

'I say, if we working men are ever to get a man's share, we must have universal suffrage, and annual parliaments, and the vote by ballot, and electoral districts.'   Ch. 30

Felix's reply to this is profounder. He suggests that these demands are not enough, and when asked to say how the working man will gain power, he replies:

'I'll tell you what's the greatest power under heaven,' said Felix, 'and that is public opinion—the ruling belief in society about what is right and what is wrong, what is honourable and what is shameful.'   Ch. 30

and he goes on to make it clear that democracy is useless in circumstances where the electorate is too ignorant to know what it is voting about. This, overall, sounds like the author herself, and certainly Felix Holt, with his large Ideality (Ch. 5), is one of her least successful characters. It is very difficult to suppose that given his background and his upbringing he would have acquired both such intense moral fervour and such articulacy.

The good things he stands for are not easily found in a single human being, and this may be why he fails. His influence over Esther is equally abstract, drawing her from a shallow frivolity to a serious regard for important things, although she herself is much more convincing.

CONCLUSION

The novels discussed in this chapter all have qualities of greatness, and by the time she was writing *Felix Holt*, George Eliot had acquired a much more relaxed command of her style. Her editorial intrusions are handled more carefully, and increasingly dispensed with, and *Felix Holt* especially is animated with a relaxed humour in the handling of such characters as the Debarrys. Each of her major novels has contributed some characteristic towards the creation of *Middlemarch*. *Adam Bede* the presentation of a rural society, *The Mill on the Floss* the presentation of an urban society and a much more complex sensibility, *Romola* the handling of a story on the grand scale, and *Felix Holt* the applying of this achievement to an English setting, and the handling of an involved story, as well as the presentation in a fully rounded way of English characters of great variety and individuality. George Eliot's achievement is totally cumulative. Each of her novels depends on the one before for an advance in skill and control. *Middlemarch* brings her past experience to a fruitful conclusion. *Daniel Deronda* represents a further experiment, when a lesser writer might have rested content, and in concept if not in performance is just as great.

7

'Middlemarch'

It is not very easy to write about masterpieces. The commentator would prefer to stand in awe and wonder. It is particularly difficulty to treat *Middlemarch* adequately within the scope of a short introduction to George Eliot's work, because while her earlier novels require and deserve serious critical attention and themselves stand up well to comparison with the major works of other authors, *Middlemarch* is a much greater achievement. Its greatness lies in the sense of reality that the world and people of Middlemarch have, the intricate organisation of its four stories which provide again and again parallels and contrasts of situation and behaviour, with a richness and control that does not exist in most other English novels, and the conviction and authority with which the characters are analysed by speech, action, and direct comment. In this chapter it will only be possible to deal with some facets of the novel, and in any case fuller studies are numerous at all levels. Professor Daiches's account of the novel (see Reading List) is clear and comprehensive, and his final paragraph suggests precisely the nature of the critical problem:

> In the end, *Middlemarch* resists formulation. Some attempt has been made here to suggest the moral ideas around which the action is constructed and the interweaving fates of the characters developed. But the novel is richer than any moral formula. There are contradictions in it, but they are contradictions and not confusions; they suggest the richness and many-sidedness of life and the different sorts of norms with reference to which life can be illuminatingly presented. 'Illumination' is perhaps the key word. *Middlemarch* illuminates experience as much today as it ever did.   p. 69

His introduction to *Middlemarch* is also valuable as an introduction to the whole of George Eliot's work, since he deals in passing with many important characteristics of her work in general. He pays particular attention to the power of her imagery in directing the reader towards the intended judgment of a character. This is a facet of her skill which requires close attention in all her novels and has only received fleeting references here.

STRUCTURE

The first stage in an appreciation of *Middlemarch* must be the grasp of its structure, which is by no means the loosely related set of stories, simply unified by being set in one district, that it has been said to consist of. Certainly, the underlying general purpose of the novel is indicated in the subtitle, *A Study of Provincial Life*. The novel is about life in a provincial town at the time just before the First Reform Bill, but it is very far from being merely a description of some people and events there. Broadly speaking it tells of the attitudes and presumptions of a whole range of social units, all interrelated, and all based in or around Middlemarch, when confronted with a variety of testing circumstances and characters. One of these characters is Dorothea Brooke, who although she belongs to the area is an orphan and has been educated abroad, as well as possessing a temperament which makes her 'different from other women'. The other three main characters who create the test are all outsiders, Lydgate the doctor, Bulstrode the banker, and Ladislaw, the who-knows-what.

THE STORIES

It is a simplification to identify the four main strands of the novel as four stories, as they are all related and interlinked, but it is helpful at first to show quickly the breadth of the novel.

The least prominent story is that of Fred Vincy and Mary Garth. Fred, the son of the Mayor of Middlemarch, is expected to rise above his father's station as a merchant, and has been educated accordingly; but he is not fitted for the higher life and eventually takes a decision to work under the estate manager,

Caleb Garth. Fred is weak in many ways, especially in his grasp of money. He squanders what he has and causes the Garths some distress before he eventually makes his decision. His love for Mary is a childhood love, but true nevertheless, and she helps to raise him to self-discipline and work. She is one of the characters in the book for whom one feels that George Eliot has an almost unreserved regard, and although she is much simpler, she is perhaps a version of Marian Evans as she might have been, especially as Garth is certainly a portrait of Robert Evans. Mary, like her creator, reads Scott, and has the same sense of humour which allows her to smile at folly without condoning it. Mary is admirably correct in her behaviour when Feather-stone asks her to burn his second will (Ch. 33) and she is rewarded because although at first she seems to have deprived Fred of an inheritance of ten thousand pounds, it is made clear later by Mr. Farebrother that even if she had burnt the second will, the first one would have been contested (Ch. 52). In any case, it is obviously better for Fred that he should not have received the money, since it is after this that he changes his ways and turns in the direction which eventually leads to his marriage to Mary.

The connections to this story, the Garth family and the Farebrothers, clearly represent for George Eliot a norm of good behaviour in the most general sense which runs quietly along behind the grander dramas. The story of Fred and Mary never reaches the level of drama, partly because they have not the temperament for it, but also because when it might, a crisis is deflected either by the restraint and good sense of Mary's parents, as in the incident when Fred comes to say he cannot repay the loan (Ch. 24), or by the more powerful and unselfish restraint of Mr. Farebrother, who not only gives up Mary, but helps Fred to win her. Much of this might have been sentimental in a novel exclusively devoted to this one story, but in the wider and richer context it is totally absorbed and made convincing.

The leading story of the novel is that of Dorothea Brooke and her two marriages, both equally distressing to most of her society, but not to her. In a state of completely unawakened idealism, she marries the middle-aged would-be scholar Edward

Casaubon. During their marriage, she realises that he is not what she thought he was. The study of their gradual awakening from the illusions on which their attraction to each other is based forms the backbone of the first half of the novel, and is most sympathetically handled. The author does not withdraw her sympathy from Casaubon, despite the littleness of his character, nor is she indulgent towards Dorothea, whose blindness (literally hinted at in her real short-sightedness) is equally closely examined. As the horror of her situation dawns on her, she meets Casaubon's cousin, Will Ladislaw, who is young and attractive. Casaubon's meanness of mind leads him to suspect a clandestine understanding between them, and as an act of spite he writes into his will a clause to the effect that if Dorothea marries Will after his death, she will lose her inheritance. This creates a fatal barrier between her and Ladislaw, which is only broken at the end by the influence of certain other strenuous events.

The third story, which is closely linked to that of Dorothea, is the story of the doctor, Lydgate, and Fred Vincy's sister Rosamond. This is in a way the easiest of the three stories. Lydgate is a doctor of the new world of serious scientific medicine rather than of quackery. He has high ideals and ambitions, and is not readily accepted in the traditional world of Middlemarch. He gains, with some doubts, the patronage of the banker Bulstrode, and achieves some highly successful cures, particularly of Fred Vincy when he has typhoid. He has already met and noticed Rosamond, but it is during this time that he becomes engaged to her. He has not much better understanding of women than he has of furniture (Ch. 15), despite his earlier entanglement in France, and he completely fails to see what is wrong for him with Rosamond's character. (Chapter 15 which tells Lydgate's past history always seems to me to be the least well-digested part of the whole novel, not so much in what it describes, but in being such a solid lump of unbroken narrative.) Rosamond has no better view of Lydgate than that he has aristocratic connections, and their marriage slowly disintegrates as the illusions each had of the other are removed. Rosamond is in fact positively perverse and is almost entirely responsible for Lydgate's failure, especially in her extravagance, and then in her foolish disobedience. She goes out riding on a rough horse while she is pregnant and so loses her baby. She tells Will Ladislaw about Casaubon's will, when her husband has expressly advised her not to, and she does so out of the merest superficial jealousy. She prevents the successful sale of their house, and she writes to Lydgate's uncle, Sir Godwin, asking for money, which causes great offence. She is like Casaubon in the littleness of her mind, and Lydgate, like Dorothea, has to accept the limitations of the person he has chosen, because she is what she is, and it was his choice. Although it is no simple restoration of her first freedom, Dorothea is released by the death of her husband, whereas the Lydgates remain together, and his aspirations are never realised. The similarities and differences of these two stories provide the most prominent structural theme in the novel.

The fourth story is that of the exposure of the banker Bulstrode, and is rather more conventional. It is bound to the other three by its consequences, for Bulstrode is connected with Lydgate, and with Ladislaw, and with the Vincys; it is a story of failure as are the stories of Casaubon and Lydgate, but its details are less involved with the other three, and one feels this strongly at the end of the novel, when Bulstrode and his wife are left alone. Whereas such as Dorothea and Farebrother are there to help Lydgate out of his difficulties, to some extent at least, there is no one who can help Bulstrode, or even thinks of it. It is in fact vaguely interesting to consider a meeting between Bulstrode and Dorothea after Bulstrode's exposure. Bulstrode is a hypocrite. His money was originally acquired from criminal activities, since he married the wealthy widow of a Jewish pawnbroker who was also a receiver of stolen goods. And he has adjusted his mind to this by an almost arithmetical balancing of his spiritual books. He is a banker after all, in the religious sense. He has convinced himself that his pursuit of good works and his puritanical life will stand in the balance against his acceptance of tainted money, and his hiding of the knowledge that his first wife's daughter was still alive and should have inherited from her. Fate pursues him in an extraordinary way, but convincing nevertheless. After Featherstone's death, there appears briefly in Middlemarch his illegitimate son, Joshua Rigg, to whom he has left the house Stone Court. Rigg, whose standards of life are not high, has an acquaintance, Raffles, married in fact to Rigg's mother, who visits him at Stone Court, and is not favourably received. Later, after Rigg has sold Stone Court to Bulstrode, Raffles returns, this time to encounter Bulstrode himself, whose past he knows of. By a series of chance encounters, Bulstrode's past and his connection with Ladislaw emerge to Middlemarch society, leading to his eventual public shaming at a meeting of the town worthies to discuss the problem arising from a case of cholera. The only strained incident in the exposure is the fact that Raffles chattered about Bulstrode in an inn in Bilkley, some forty miles away, and was overheard by a Middlemarch man, Bainbridge. Thus, despite what Bulstrode has gone through to keep his past quiet, it still leaks out. This is not really an unlikely coincidence—in fact highly probable, compared with many novelist's manipulations—but it is prepared for a little self-consciously, when Bulstrode going through Raffles's pockets for incriminating evidence finds the bill from the inn in Bilkley.

The relationships between the four stories are too numerous to mention. They occur in incidents, in situations and in themes. The parallel between Dorothea's marriage and Lydgate's has been mentioned, and between Bulstrode, Lydgate and Casaubon, as failures, contrasted with Fred Vincy as an unpredictable success. Casaubon is also linked to Bulstrode in that both owe a debt to Ladislaw, since neither would be rich if he had his true inheritance. There are also characters who create narrative links, especially Farebrother who links Lydgate and Dorothea, Featherstone who links the Vincys and Bulstrode and the Garths, and Raffles, who surprisingly links Bulstrode with Ladislaw. This connection is the one which binds the whole novel in a set of family relationships, as will be shown below.

NARRATIVE CONSTRUCTION

After we have identified the four main threads we can learn a good deal from the narrative method of the novel. It is unnecessary to discuss how George Eliot handles the chronology of it. We have already seen her learning how to vary her time-schemes, and to move about in time and space. In *Middlemarch*, she does it very unobtrusively. The novel runs from the autumn of 1829 to the summer of 1832, but within that time George Eliot moves backwards and forwards according to her needs. An analysis of this would reveal more contrasts and balances of theme and character.

It is a slightly less mechanical exercise to study how she balances the narrative. There are two focal centres deriving in fact from the two original stories out of which the novel was made. They are the arena of Tipton, Freshitt and Lowick, which centres on Dorothea, and the arena of Middlemarch which has no clear centre except perhaps Mr. Vincy, the Mayor, though that is not to suggest that he holds a central place. It is simply that Fred is his son, Rosamond his daughter, and Harriet Bulstrode his sister.

George Eliot handles these two centres in an illuminating way. The novel opens by concentrating on Dorothea, her family, and her immediate concerns. This allows the reader to establish himself, and to get to know well a manageable part of the setting. The first ten chapters deal with Dorothea and Casaubon, and the reactions to her choice. In Chapter 10 Middlemarch comes to Tipton, which allows the author to shift the emphasis. From Chapter 11 to Chapter 18 the emphasis is on the Middlemarch people and introduces the Vincys, the Garths and the Feather-stones, as well as Lydgate.

After these two long sections, the shifts become more frequent, as we see the Casaubons in Rome, then the fortunes of the Vincys, the return of Casaubon and his illness, and Featherstone's death. These four stages are balanced against each other, and bring us to the end of Book Three. In Books Four and Five, the stories begin to merge and connect, following the consequences of Featherstone's death, and the plans of Mr. Brooke to go in for politics, with Ladislaw as editor of a local journal, *The Pioneer*, writing for him on the Liberal cause. George Eliot begins in Book Four, Chapter 37, to make the shifts of focus within a single chapter. We hear the reactions of Middlemarchers to Brooke's intentions, and then shift to Will and Dorothea at Tipton. In Book Five the shifts cease to be so relevant, because Dorothea's and Lydgate's stories are moving together, especially as Ladislaw is friendly with the Lydgates. I shall analyse some chapters from this very important Book later.

Books Six and Seven concentrate chiefly on the affairs of Bulstrode and Lydgate, with only occasional excursions to the other arena. This is partly because the novel is moving to its climax in the exposing of Bulstrode, on which the conclusion of all the other stories depends, and partly because Will and Dorothea have separated, and their fortunes seem to be inevitably apart. Only three chapters in Book Six show us Dorothea, and all deal with her separation from Will; she does not figure at all in Book Seven, except right at the end, with some dramatic force, when she hears of Lydgate's disgrace and refuses to accept it. This produces a sudden reversal of emphasis. Apart from a few chapters on the Bulstrodes the whole of Book Eight concentrates on Dorothea, Lydgate, Rosamond and Ladislaw, and the concluding of their fortunes as far as we are concerned. And Dorothea becomes again the central character as she was in Book One.

This handling of the focus shows as well as anything the great controlled sweep of the novel.

The Separate Books

The titles of the eight books of the novel are useful guides to the author's main intentions. Book One is called obviously enough 'Miss Brooke', through whom we are led on to the rest of Middlemarch society. Book Two is called 'Old and Young', and treats of the sense of failed communication between the elderly Casaubon and his twenty-year-old bride, illuminated by their contact with Ladislaw and his friend Naumann, both not only young but youthful in manner too. This is compared with the generation contrast in Middlemarch between Feather-stone, Bulstrode, his wife and Vincy, and on the other hand Fred and Mary, and Lydgate and Rosamond. The pattern in

Book Three, 'Waiting for Death', is more pointed. The death that is waited for is Featherstone's, but it is in this book that Casaubon falls ill, and his death becomes a possibility, which might well be waited for with some hope. Furthermore, Fred might have died of typhoid if Lydgate had not been there, while, as a contrast, it is in this context that Lydgate and Rosamond become engaged.

In Book Four the three love problems are those of Fred and Mary which arises from his low expectations, and also because of Farebrother; Dorothea's and Will's because although Casaubon has forbidden Will to come, Brooke has invited him to stay at Tipton, an event which Casaubon sees as a connivance; and Lydgate's and Rosamond's because of the different attitude of the Vincys to the forthcoming marriage from Lydgate's own. Every aspect of each problem is different.

Book Five is called 'The Dead Hand', which refers to Casaubon's influence on Dorothea after his death. However, it is also the book in which Raffles meets Bulstrode, which is an accidental consequence of the dead hand of Featherstone. Back in Chapter 34 the phrase is used in connection with Featherstone, who for all his malicious plots to annoy his dependents after his death, could hardly have thought up anything as satisfying to himself as this accidental means of bringing Nemesis to Bulstrode.

Book Six is called 'The Widow and the Wife', which refers chiefly to Dorothea and Rosamond, though here again it is worth noticing that it might apply ironically to Bulstrode's past. He made a widow his wife, as is told in this book, and that was the root of his temporary success and ultimate collapse.

'The Two Temptations' in Book Seven are those of Lydgate to ignore the implications of Bulstrode's change of mind over the loan, and Bulstrode's much worse one in contriving the death of Raffles by allowing his servant to give the man alcohol, expressly against Lydgate's wishes. But there are other links here. Lydgate also succumbs to the temptation of gambling and drugs, the sort of thing which had been disapproved of in Farebrother, while Farebrother does not succumb to any selfish temptation and carries through his determination to renounce

Mary. Similarly, Garth refuses to manage Bulstrode's business, having heard of his past from Raffles. This is not hard for Garth, whose strictness in such matters tends to self-righteousness, but it is nevertheless another part of his desires to take charge of as many local and adjacent properties as he can for the sake of better management. Garth's harshness to Bulstrode is incidentally the major means whereby George Eliot forces the reader to sympathise with Bulstrode, and is a good example of her objectivity. Garth is one of the characters to whom she has been supposed to be over-indulgent.

The final book is called 'Sunset and Sunrise', and although there are several possible applications of this—the end of Bulstrode, and the beginning of the end of Lydgate, alongside the start of a new life for Dorothea and Ladislaw being the obvious ones—it also implies the larger theme of the endless continuum of life. George Eliot ties up the future lives of the main characters neatly and on the whole pleasantly for us, in the expected manner of the Victorians, but she must have been above all aware that what she was doing was no more than a gesture. As every situation reaches some sort of end, so another begins. George Eliot knew well enough that the gradual process of change which she charted in Middlemarch was to go on, that the Vincys and Garths, and the Chettams and Cadwalladers would have to face just as much in the years to come, both in social and political change as well as the timeless tragedies and comedies of life. And she also knew well the London life which the Lydgates and Ladislaws go into. All this is hinted at in the title of the last book, despite the soothing security of the Epilogue.

RELATIONSHIPS

All the major characters of the story are connected either by blood or marriage. This does not at first, of course, seem at all probable, but when the Ladislaw story is unfolded and the connection between Bulstrode and Ladislaw revealed, the final link is made. The Middlemarch group is quite easily linked. Bulstrode's wife is Vincy's sister. Mrs. Vincy's sister was Featherstone's first wife, and his second wife was Mrs. Garth's sister.

All that is fairly predictable in the provincial Middlemarch society. The link from the Brookes via the Casaubons to Ladislaw and hence to Bulstrode is more obscure. The two tables which follow may help to explain the relationships to a reader of the novel and will also help to demonstrate how Ladislaw is twice disinherited.

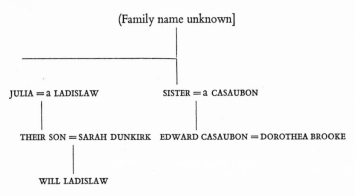

When Casaubon's Aunt Julia, whose picture Dorothea sees at Tipton, runs away with the 'Polish dancing-master', she is disinherited, which is how Edward Casaubon acquires his fortune.

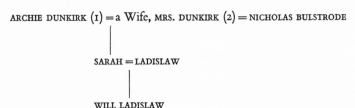

Sarah Dunkirk also leaves home, because her father is a pawn-broker and receiver of stolen goods. Mrs. Dunkirk inherits, but later leaves the money away from the family to her second husband, Bulstrode, who leaves London when she dies, and settles in Middlemarch where he marries Vincy's sister Harriet.

It is this complexity in Ladislaw's background that allows Mrs. Cadwallader to comment so unfavourably on him, since he is compounded of Casaubon, whom she has little time for, the Polish 'dancing-master' as she puts it, and the Jewish pawn-broker. Actually this background is extremely important to one of the general themes of the novel, as we shall see.

THE SOCIAL SCALE

It is in the incorporation of all areas of Middlemarch society that George Eliot is so skilful, for this is by no means an obvious or self-conscious aspect of the novel as it is in *Bleak House* or *The Canterbury Tales*. She works into the novel different elements of the rural society around the town—the Chettams, the Cadwalladers, Brooke himself, as well as the cameo of the poor farmer, Dagley. This is the old world of complacency which is about to be moved, but the figures are no mere types. Sir James Chettam is kept sympathetic because of Celia, but is also rebuked not only by Dorothea, but also by Cadwallader, when his aristocratic bigotry threatens to become absurd, and while he is more pompous he is much less ridiculous than Brooke, the Liberal.

The church is represented by Casaubon—the scholarly land-owning cleric, whose work in his parish is limited to the Sunday sermon, and not even that every week; Farebrother, a human figure reminiscent of Mr. Irwine in *Adam Bede*; and Bulstrode, who while not ordained is more precisely strict than any. There are also references to others.

In Middlemarch too we meet a wide range of people, from the rich and miserly landowner Featherstone, through such professional figures as Vincy the merchant, Bulstrode the banker, Standish the lawyer, Trumbull the auctioneer, and a whole range of doctors, and then the Garths, as well as various minor figures from more dubious walks of life, though it is not part of George Eliot's intention to delve into the mire of 19th-century town life, which perhaps indicates how her purpose is not either firstly or even mainly a social one. She has no axe to grind about the social calamities of the Industrial Revolution, though she is rather stronger about bad doctors and the corruptions of electioneering.

What is very gradually revealed during the novel is the slow process of changing attitudes as the provincial society becomes eroded by external influences. Of these Bulstrode is less important from this point of view, for it has been his main purpose to show that he is a traditional member of the society, and not an upstart whose money is tainted. The ones that matter are Lydgate and Ladislaw, and it is, of course, indicative that they are the two main characters who leave Middlemarch at the end. So does Bulstrode, but he is cut out, like a diseased organ, much in the same way as Middlemarch is cleared of cholera. Lydgate and Ladislaw go away because it is not the place for them, but they do leave behind very slight marks, Lydgate on the medical profession, Ladislaw on the old rural world, and each takes with him a daughter of the old world. Ladislaw, more than anyone else, represents the nature of the change. He is rootless, and he is also an exotic mixture as far as his blood goes. He wants to be free but he does not lack confidence. He is secure in his expectation of falling on his feet. He is contradictory in his moral standpoints but this is most likely a consequence of his rootlessness, and something which George Eliot intends. He has at times a flavour of Tito Melema, but he does not go the same way. He and Dorothea are successful in their London life and one feels that this is not just a matter of tying up the loose ends. While George Eliot must have seen that their marriage too might have ended in tragedy, for Will is light with his favours and Dorothea jealous, she surely saw them as the type of new people which she could admire. It is this feature of *Middlemarch* which anticipates *Daniel Deronda*. Middlemarch also represents George Eliot's most complete picture of the old world which had preoccupied her for so long, and the setting of *Daniel Deronda* in her own recent times was an almost inevitable consequence.

It is the richness of the social scale represented in *Middlemarch* that contributes to one of its characteristics, which is something that only occurs in works of this stature: the capacity to invest an almost trivial incident with wider importance, and do it with a light touch. Almost at the end of the novel, just after she has surprised Rosamond with Ladislaw, Dorothea goes to Freshitt Hall to tell Sir James what she has learnt from Lydgate. Celia comments on her state of excitement:

'Dodo, how very bright your eyes are!' said Celia, when Sir James was gone out of the room. 'And you don't see anything you look at, Arthur or anything. You are going to do something uncomfortable, I know. Is it all about Mr. Lydgate, or has something else happened?' Celia had been used to watch her sister with expectation.

'Yes, dear, a great many things have happened,' said Dodo, in her full tones.

'I wonder what,' said Celia, folding her arms cozily and leaning forward on them.

'Oh, all the troubles of all people on the face of the earth,' said Dorothea, lifting her arms to the back of her head.

'Dear me, Dodo, are you going to have a scheme for them?' said Celia, a little uneasy at this Hamlet-like raving.

This passage is charged with effect, though its actual force is not so easy to pin down. Celia's comical naïvety is both comforting and irritating. Dorothea's irony is both true and yet typically inflated—the allusion to Hamlet is pertinent—and the use of the name Dodo, which is comically deflating, adds another touch to the scene which prevents it from becoming solemn or portentous.

CHAPTERS 51–54

Any selection of specific chapters in *Middlemarch* for comment does not necessarily imply that they are better than others; but these four chapters from Books Five and Six show in one way how the rich construction of the novel works.

Chapter 51 records Mr. Brooke's speech with all its commentary on electioneering corruption—a scene of action, humour and direct social relevance. Its consequences which were mostly predictable also have bearing on Ladislaw. Brooke, seeing a means of gratifying Chettam's view that Ladislaw should be got rid of, indicates that he will give up *The Pioneer*.

Ladislaw is not inclined to take the hint, indeed quite the reverse. He says to himself:

'I shall stay as long as I like. I shall go of my own movement and not because they are afraid of me.'

This is then passed over until Chapter 54 in which Ladislaw goes to say good-bye to Dorothea. At the end of their interview, the same idea reappears, but it is transmuted, rather like a phrase of music in a symphony. It has changed key. Where in the first case it was a superficial temperamental reaction to an immediate situation, a fairly forgivable moment of pride in the face of bigotry, it is now much more serious and applies to both characters. Dorothea says:

> 'Sorrow comes in so many ways. Two years ago I had no notion of that—I mean of the unexpected ways in which trouble comes, and ties our hands, and makes us silent when we long to speak. I used to despise women a little for not shaping their lives more, and doing better things. I was very fond of doing as I liked, but I have almost given it up,' she ended, smiling playfully.
> 'I have not given up doing as I like, but I can very seldom do it,' said Will. Ch. 54

This has two levels itself. Firstly, they are in love, but cannot say so, or even allow themselves to think it. Then they are also both independent persons, used to relying on their own wills, who have been contained by the behaviour of people lesser than themselves.

Between these two closely-linked episodes come the chapters in which Farebrother receives the Lowick living from Dorothea, but at the same time is asked by Fred Vincy to go to Mary Garth to find out what his chances are. Neither Fred nor Mary is aware that Farebrother himself is in love with Mary. Here is a good man walled in by his society, with no chance of escape, and yet weathering a situation as hard on himself as that.

Then follows the chapter in which Bulstrode first encounters Raffles, into which is also built the fact that Garth knows his history, but will not reveal it.

In four successive chapters, in four critical events, several of the main characters experience a crisis—Brooke, Ladislaw, Farebrother, Mary Garth, Bulstrode and Dorothea. The novel can only sustain this sequence of events because the world it evokes is so convincing, and because the total scope and slow

and comforts him, the whole of the passage (Ch. 66) is shot through with a type of enthusiasm which is not currently popular and is not at all tinged with protective irony as it would be today, and it is rather more true that George Eliot stresses the fact of Dorothea's womanliness in a way that detracts from what she is actually doing. (It is interesting to observe that George Eliot obviously saw the unsatisfactory element of this and consequently translated Dorothea into a man in her next novel. In this century it would have been easier for her to show that what she was trying to identify was a basic human value to which the distinction between the sexes was irrelevant.) But throughout the last Book, George Eliot takes care to remain selfconsciously detached from 'poor Mrs. Casaubon' and is perfectly well aware that the naïvety of her character's idealism is a quality that could well cause it to be of no avail.

Dorothea's reward for her generosity towards Lydgate is, in the weaving of chance, to find herself forlorn and convinced that she has lost Ladislaw, but her subsequent further encounter with Rosamond shows just how clearly George Eliot believed in what she was trying to make Dorothea stand for—the power of goodwill. In the presence of Dorothea, Rosamond tells the truth about herself and Ladislaw, against herself in a quite untypical way—just as Hetty tells the truth to Dinah, and Gwendolen is raised beyond herself by Daniel Deronda. If art must be perfectly crystalline and lucid, then this dominant element of all George Eliot's novels might be seen as a fault or flaw, but perhaps it is more proper to the art of the novel than to any other art to contain the whole ambiguity of the human condition, even if the result evokes an ambiguous response. In this latter part of *Middlemarch*, George Eliot is moving towards her last novel, and an understanding of that is as important to an understanding of *Middlemarch* as any reading of the earlier novels.

8

Into the New World

On 25 January 1876 George Eliot wrote to Joseph Payne an often-quoted letter, which is one of the best descriptions of her work:

> My writing is simply a set of experiments in life—an endeavour to see what our thought and emotion may be capable of—what stores of motive, actual or hinted as possible, give promise of a better after which we may strive—what gains from past revelations and discipline we must strive to keep hold of as something more sure than shifting theory. I become more and more timid—with less daring to adopt any formula which does not get itself clothed for me in some human figure and individual experience, and perhaps that is a sign that if I help others to see at all it must be through that medium of art.

Some of her characters are the consequences of these experiments, especially the ones which have in them some idea or feeling which gives promise of a better world. This is the basic problem of Felix Holt and Dorothea Brooke. Both have ideals which are better than those we have. The fact that they raise doubts in readers' minds about their success as characters indicates rather well how far their ideals are beyond the experience of most readers, as real experiences, despite the fact that many would agree with them in theory. Dorothea is the most convincing, because what she achieves is in the realm of the possible, and she is held in check by those who surround her.

Daniel Deronda presents the most difficult case of all. In fact our appreciation of the novel probably depends on our acceptance of Daniel Deronda as a representative, a symbolic figure both in his search for his origins, and his espousal of the Jewish cause, as well as in his role of confessor to Gwendolen. It is too easy to fault him as a real character. He is too good, he has more wisdom than we can believe in, he is like a sage from a science-fiction novel or a fantasy, whose wisdom is a consequence of centuries of experience stored in the collective conscious. If we accept him in that light, then the novel becomes easier. He belongs with Sir Henry Harcourt-Reilly in *The Cocktail Party* to that special band who are endowed with unusual insight. George Eliot actually hints at this from time to time, though she shies away from it elsewhere, and concentrates on his ordinariness.

> He was conscious of that peculiar irritation which will sometimes befall the man whom others are inclined to trust as a mentor—the irritation of perceiving that he is supposed to be entirely off the same plane of desire and temptation as those who confess to him.
> Ch. 37

In the same chapter, too, she draws attention to his unusual sensibility and his absence of a close friend. He is a man apart. But he is not treated purely as that and there lies the problem.

The novel *Daniel Deronda* is not much read. It is more difficult to read and understand than *Middlemarch*, and it moves not only into a completely new sphere for its setting and its type of character, and one which is not likely to attract the English reader very much, but also it tackles a problem which now as then provokes reactions that are not quite straightforward, the problem of the place of the Jews. It is a much more sombre and pessimistic novel than any other of hers. Gwendolen Harleth is deprived of all comfort and left desolate. The novel is constructed of two stories which do not blend as do the strands of *Middlemarch*, although they are full of the same sort of contrasts and parallels.

It is possible to approach it in the same way as *Middlemarch*, that is to analyse its component parts and its narrative method, but this approach is less rewarding, for the book is not such a tight organism, nor does it have the same grand rise and fall of the earlier novel. In the context of this study I shall approach it from two viewpoints: firstly that it deals with exceptional rather than ordinary people, secondly that it deals with George Eliot's contemporaries rather than with the period of or before her childhood.

THE EXCEPTIONAL

Throughout the greater part of her creative life, George Eliot dealt with ordinary people. She raised this banner straight away in *Amos Barton*. There is no gifted person in that story. She avoided characters with exceptional gifts in all the other prose works except *Romola*, although there are in them some characters who are not quite ordinary, especially Felix Holt and Dorothea. In *Daniel Deronda* she has unpredictably and very greatly altered the type of character she is studying. The majority of the major characters of the novel are not at all ordinary. They are extra-ordinary, or at least exceptional in their fields. Very few novelists attempt to create geniuses in their fiction—it is held to be one of the most difficult things to do convincingly, and yet in a manner of speaking, there are four or five persons in *Daniel Deronda* who might be given that title.

Clearly George Eliot would have understood the word 'genius', which is really very vague, to mean an extraordinary or exceptional person. The most obvious of these is Klesmer, whose power is evoked in only three or four scenes. His precise musical genius is not dwelt on, but simply understood. What is brought out is the force of his whole personality, first in his dealings with the Arrowpoints—one of George Eliot's most memorable comic scenes—then in the scene in which he takes Gwendolen's pretensions to an acting career to pieces with passionate incisiveness, a scene which demonstrates his dedication to art, and finally and more lightly in the scene when he hears and acknowledges Mirah's musical ability. In this last scene, especially, the sense of his being a 'great man' is most strongly created by the contrast with the 'ordinary' Meyricks (Chs. 22, 23, 39).

Also in the context of music is Daniel's mother, called the Alcharisi, again not only an outstanding singer, but an extraordinary personality, possessed with a passionate distaste for the Jewish cause that her father stood for and anxious to keep her son from it, but defeated in the end, by what one can only call Destiny. It is plainly Daniel's destiny to encounter both Mirah and Mordecai as he does, and eventually to discover his real heritage. George Eliot is not so naïve by this time, if she ever was, as to suppose that we will accept these encounters as merely random events in a lottery world. This is another development in this novel—the scale of human destiny is enlarged to take in greater movements of consciousness than for example the simple retributive consequences that pursue Bulstrode. What happens in *Middlemarch* is the result of personal characteristics combining with each other and within a social framework to produce certain understandable consequences, and the pattern of historical development is very much in the background, and is in any case only a slight one. *Daniel Deronda* looks backwards and forwards in history, linking the Old Testament Jews with Spanish Jewry, with the movement in George Eliot's own lifetime and on to modern Israel. *Middlemarch*, for all its grandeur, is not written on that scale. Again, the author is looking at the extraordinary.

Mordecai too is extraordinary. How many novelists have attempted to create a convincing portrayal of a prophet? I should add that I am not assuming that either Klesmer, or Alcharisi, or Mordecai are wholly successful, but I am implying that in the terms of this particular novel, it does not matter so much. They operate as symbols of particular types of greatness in the arena of the human spirit. What of Mordecai's visionary convictions about Daniel? Do we believe in them? Probably not. But we believe that Mordecai believes in them, and certainly this type of superstitious faith is by no means the prerogative of the Jews.

The remaining two extraordinary characters must be treated differently. They are not possessed of any exceptional talents in any given field, but are nevertheless most unusual personalities. It is constantly claimed that where Daniel is a failure as a character, Grandcourt is a success. It is not so often observed that both are extraordinary. One is extraordinarily good and wise, the other is extraordinarily bad and clever. One encounters Mirah, who is susceptible to the elevating power of his goodness; the other encounters Gwendolen, who is susceptible to the degrading power of his badness. She likes it. That is why she marries him. He does not offend her frigidity, which we have been shown in her dealings with Rex Gascoigne. The crisis of the novel lies in the obligation which destiny also imposes on Daniel to attempt to raise and strengthen Gwendolen, without deserting his higher commitment.

The pattern in *Daniel Deronda* works itself out in a remarkable way, and as in the encounters between Daniel and Mirah by the river, and Daniel and Mordecai on the bridge, it invites the charge of unrealistic and therefore unacceptable staging.

It is of course extraordinary (in keeping with the whole concept of the novel) that Daniel should be meeting his mother in Genoa, at exactly the same time that Grandcourt has to put in there with his yacht for repairs. But George Eliot does not pretend that it is anything else. There is a splendid comic paragraph in which Grandcourt finds himself fantastically thwarted in his attempts to separate Gwendolen and Daniel. Destiny, and it cannot be anything else, is too strong for him, as he must grudgingly admit. The Grandcourts meet Deronda on the staircase of their hotel:

> There was a start of surprise in Deronda before he could raise his hat and pass on. The moment did not seem to favour any closer greeting, and the circumstances under which they had last parted made him doubtful whether Grandcourt would be civilly inclined to him.
>
> [This is an ironical understatement as far as the meaning of the occasion for the Grandcourts goes, though it is surely Daniel's real thought, for Gwendolen has never been, nor ever will be, at the front of Daniel's mind, except during her crisis shortly to come.]
>
> The doubt might certainly have been changed into a disagreeable certainty, for Grandcourt, on this unaccountable appearance of Deronda at Genoa of all places, immediately tried to conceive how there could have been an arrangement between him and Gwendolen.

It is true that before they were well in their rooms, he had seen how difficult it was to shape such an arrangement with any probability, being too cool-headed to find it at once easily credible that Gwendolen had not only while in London hastened to inform Deronda of the yachting project, but had posted a letter to him from Marseilles or Barcelona, advising him to travel to Genoa in time for the chance of meeting her there or of receiving a letter from her telling of some other destination—all which must have implied some miraculous foreknowledge in her, and in Deronda a bird-like facility in flying about and perching idly.   Ch. 54

The author is laughing out loud at Grandcourt here, though he is by no means a comic character in his influence, and it is almost inevitable that she should kill him off very quickly afterwards. There is a kind of novelistic delight about the whole situation.

If there is any doubt that the novel is dealing with the extra-ordinary and exceptional, in direct contrast with everything she has done before, there are various occasions when the author uses these words, for instance in connection, not with the five charac-ters so far mentioned as exceptional, but with the two girls. Of Mirah:

> Her *peculiar* life and education had produced in her an *extraordinary* mixture of unworldliness, with knowledge of the world's evil.
> (My italics) Ch. 52

Of Gwendolen:

> 'Then she is not much like the rest of her sex; that's all I can say,' said Sir Hugo, with a slight shrug. 'However, she ought to be some-thing *extraordinary*, for there must be an entanglement between your horoscope and hers—eh?'   Ch. 59

This quotation is less pertinent in one way because Sir Hugo is partial, but it is relevant nonetheless and also indicates George Eliot's consciousness of what her construction is intended to show. Sir Hugo tends to represent the ordinary view of these rather extraordinary events. He, for example, is rather shocked by Grandcourt's will, whereas Deronda, and also Gwendolen, believe that whatever the motive, Grandcourt has done the right thing by his and Lydia Glasher's son. This is a moral viewpoint that Sir Hugo hardly comprehends, and he does not notice the asperity of Daniel's tone (Ch. 59).

THE NEW WORLD

The most noticeable general feature of *Daniel Deronda* is that it is set between the years 1864–6, in other words within the ready memory of all its contemporary readers, and at the same time retains the feeling of great historical shaping that is more easily done with novels set at a greater distance from the time of writing. There are not many references to current European affairs, but there is one very important one. Just as Daniel goes off to meet his mother, and the Grandcourts go for their cruise, there is a fleeting reference to the Battle of Sadowa, which took place on 3 July 1866, and more than anything else marked the turning point in the unification of Germany. The novel ends at the time when Europe has become a new world in comparison with what it was in 1815, the world which in due course gave birth to the two World Wars, and the creation of the state of Israel. In that context, *Daniel Deronda* has a kind of visionary power which *Middlemarch*, despite the importance of 1832 in the history of this country, has not.

The other feature of the new world is the cosmopolitan atmosphere, and the extraordinarily varied origins of the characters. Gwendolen may be English, but she is rootless, and her maternal grandfather was a West Indian planter. Sir Hugo is English too, but he is widely travelled in Europe and is a different figure from Chettam or Brooke. Grandcourt is the only wholly English character among the main ones. And the Jews are very varied too. Klesmer is Polish, and so are the Lapidoths originally, though they have taken in most of Europe and America. The Charisis are Italian of Spanish stock. Even the Meyricks have 'streaks of eccentricity from the mother's blood as well as the father's'—she is half French, half Scot (Ch. 18). And George Eliot makes much of this when Daniel goes to Mordecai's club, where most of the members are not basically English. This conglomeration deliberately creates an atmosphere of shifting

146

rootlessness as a background for Daniel's search for an identity, and then for a cause.

There is another change too. In almost every case before this last novel, egotism leads to harm, either to others or to the egotist himself, or both, and the admired characters are those who make renunciations of selfish desires. Since creating Felix Holt, George Eliot has been studying the possibilities of harnessing egotism to some greater cause. This is what Felix and Dorothea are looking for without really finding it. Klesmer and Mordecai have both found it, and Daniel joins them in the course of the novel.

Daniel Deronda is a more schematic novel than *Middlemarch*, its characters are less realistically successful, the moral issues it raises are less subtle, the style is sometimes too intense and the matter too concentrated, but in some of the ways I have tried to suggest, it represents a great leap on its author's part into territories unexplored before.

CONCLUSION

Within an expanding pattern of realism and idealism, George Eliot explores throughout her work an immense range of convincing human situations, examining what brings them about in character and in society. She concentrates on particular intense moments of choice, but offers no clear or doctrinaire guidance. That would be no part of a novelist's art. Her imagination takes in the inner nature of any individual she creates. This is what allows her to be compassionate with all her characters. Grandcourt is the one outstanding case where she withdraws her compassion. And it takes in with equal force the external context which shapes and guides, or misleads, the inner nature. Her novels are remarkably lucid and explicit intellectually, which is a possible reason for her lesser popularity. She is *too* tough, and

> Humankind cannot bear very much reality. (T. S. Eliot: Burnt Norton)

Further Reading

This selected book list includes only works for the student approaching George Eliot for the first time. Most of her novels are readily available in cheap editions, for example Everyman, with the exception of *Scenes of Clerical Life* which is not in print.

1. Joan Bennett: *George Eliot, Her Mind and Her Art* (Cambridge University Press, 1948).
2. David Daiches: *Middlemarch* (Edward Arnold, 1963).
3. George Eliot: *Essays*, edited by Thomas Pinney (Routledge and Kegan Paul, 1963).
4. G. S. Haight: *A Century of George Eliot Criticism* (University Paperbacks, 1966).
5. G. S. Haight: *George Eliot, A Biography* (Oxford University Press, 1968). Professor Haight's biography and his collection of criticism which covers her contemporaries and present-day critics are absolutely indispensable.
6. Barbara Hardy: *The Novels of George Eliot* (Athlone, 1959).
7. Barbara Hardy (ed.): *Critical Essays on George Eliot* (Routledge and Kegan Paul, 1970).
8. W. J. Harvey: *The Art of George Eliot* (Chatto and Windus, 1961).
9. F. R. Leavis: *The Great Tradition*, 1948 (Peregrine Books, 1962). The chapter on George Eliot is included in Haight's collection of criticism, but the rest of the book is equally important for an understanding of the novel.
10. Jerome Thale: *The Novels of George Eliot* (Columbia University Press, 1959).

Index

(Titles in italics; characters in bold type)